WHAT ON EARTH IS HAPPENING!

BY TERRA KERN

WHAT ON EARTH IS HAPPENING!

BY TERRA KERN

CHAPTER ONE

THE CONTINUING VISION

PART ONE

About a year ago, as of the time of my writing this, I was given various parts of an ongoing vision for about three months straight. The first installment of the vision was of an enormous mountain covered from top to bottom in deep glistening snow. My attention was directed to the top of the mountain and there I saw activity. Right in the center of the mountaintop were two downhill skiers, knees bent, poles at their sides, and their red-and-white striped winter scarfs fluttering behind them in the wind. For a split second, I thought of 'Where's Waldo' when I spotted the scarves. Then my attention was drawn to the right. On the right side of the mountaintop, there were two snowmobilers throwing up waves of powdery snow behind them as they forged forward through the brilliantly white snow while playing on their machines. When I looked to the left side of the mountaintop, there was a group of ten people completely bundled up in winter clothing with fur-lined parkas and boots reaching up to their knees, reminding me of Eskimos. They were all connected to one another by a rope and metal clips, with all of them carrying pick axes in their thick mittened hands and half of them with large backpacks fully loaded up with gear and other provisions sitting on their backs. They reminded me of an exhibition team of mountain climbers trekking their way to the top of Mount Everest.

As I was watching the scene that was being shown to me, suddenly, I felt a slow rumble of power building, then crescendo. I don't even have the words to describe this incredible power. The nearest thing I can think of to liken it to, would be back when my husband used to race his dragster. At all the national events we participated in, there was always the class of top fuel dragsters. While being a spectator seated in the stands, I felt an atmospheric change of pressure when those babies fired up at the starting line. Then, once the amber lights of the tree dropped down to green and those machines took off rocketing down the track, I felt the power and pressure within my chest intensify in ratio to how close they were to me. At the moments they were just before me, in front of me, then just past me, the power and pressure on and within my chest was so great, that my breathing and heartbeat changed and fell in line with the rhythm of the engine's firing sequence and RPM (revolutions per minute). That's the closest thing I can think of to describe the power I felt building up as the vision unfolded before me. However, it was much more powerful than that and carried a sense of extreme seriousness.

At the moment of that rumbling crescendo of power, an avalanche began and commenced to race down the mountainside. I could do nothing except watch in awe, trepidation, and wonderment, all at the same time. While watching, an unusual sight was happening right before my eyes. As the quick moving mass of snow reached the skiers, one of them leapt high into the air and jumped right over the enormous wave of snow, landing perfectly on the mountainside behind it, continuing to downhill ski. However, the other skier was gone, he had entirely disappeared. He had been completely swept away in the avalanche.

Then my eyes were drawn to the two snowmobilers just in time to witness the powerful wave of snow curl up and over the snowmobilers. It reminded me of a surfer riding in the curl of an ocean wave. I couldn't see the snowmobilers as they rode beneath the curling snow wave, but when the snow gathered together again as a solid mass continuing its downward descent, only one snowmobiler remained behind it.

Next, my eyes were directed to the ten mountain climbers trekking toward the top of the mountain. As I watched the powerful avalanche approach, overtake, cover, and then continue its downward course, there were now only five of the ten mountain climbers left. As my attention was drawn to the five remaining hikers, I identified them as the five that had fully loaded packs upon on their backs. It was here, where the vision ended. I was completely stunned and dumbfounded. About a week later, I was given the same vision once more, complete with the power of the scene reverberating within my whole body, yet again. Since I was given the same vision twice, I knew it was of dire importance and pondered upon it often. As I did, I was reminded of several corresponding prophecies and other text from a sacred book of ancient writings I own and cherish. I'll share them with you in an upcoming chapter.

PART TWO

The second installment of the vision came about one week later. Once again, I was shown an enormous mountain, however, this time the mountain was not snow-covered, but was devoid of anything on it at all. It was the color of toffee-brown dirt and reminded me of a volcano. At the top of the mountain there were ridges from erosion with sharp, narrow peaks. All of a sudden, the mountain started shaking and I felt it throughout my whole body. I once again sensed that same intense power, that deep rumbling throughout it, resetting the rhythm of my beating heart. There was also a penetrating vibrating sensation that I could literally feel down deep and into my bones. This pulsating phenomenon reminded me of an electric powered muscle massager my grandmother once owned. When I was just a little girl, I turned it on once, holding it between my two little hands and it began vibrating, making my hands and arms rapidly shake or buzz. What I was experiencing while viewing this vision was something very similar to that, but this sensation encompassed my whole being.

I thought to myself that I was sure I was about to see molten lava spew into the air as a volcano erupted. But I was mistaken. There was most definitely an eruption, but what the mountain was spewing out wasn't molten lava at all, but very thick reddish-brown mud. I watched that mud being launched high up into clear, peaceful, azure skies with fluffy white clouds as the backdrop. Then the voluminous mud globules began to rain down on the top of the mountain and collect there. As the spewing mud got high and thick upon the mountain's top, it began to slide down faster and faster, covering more and more of the mountain as it roared down the entire mountain, not in streams like you see when a volcano erupts and the lava flows down in rivulets, but this mudslide was covering the whole mountain in real time, right before my eyes. I was observing a forceful, massive mudslide!

An ominous feeling overtook me as the beautiful skies above became dark and foreboding with flashes of lightening, both bright white and deep red, bouncing around in the blackened clouds that had gathered just over it. I wondered within my mind what was happening. But before I could contemplate over what was taking place any more, my focus was honed in on the scene, giving me a closer look with more detail. This honing in was like when one looks at a map on any type of smart screen and place their finger and thumb in a pinch position then spread them apart, zooming in closer, and getting a more detailed view. After the zooming in, as I looked at the mudslide, what I saw was terrifying. There, embedded in the fastmoving mud, were people of all sorts, both men and women stuck in mud, chest deep. Whether they were sitting or standing, I could not tell. All these people had looks of pure shock or looks of sheer fright on their faces. They were all either waving their arms frantically or had their arms out to their sides trying to stop themselves from sliding further down. But every one of their attempts were futile. They were up against a power much too strong for them to contend with, let alone overcome.

I wondered in my mind what this was and why I was being shown it. The hurricane induced mudslide in North Carolina had just taken place within the last month or so, and I was trying to figure out if this vision before me had anything to do with it, when suddenly, everything came to a complete stop. The sliding mud had reached the bottom and completely disappeared along with the people caught up in it. The strong vibrating and buzzing ceased all motion. Just then, I heard the voice of The Ancient of Days speak, "I am cleaning off the dirt from My holy mountain!" Then the vision ended. I instantly knew He had spoken to give me clarity so I wouldn't be confused and would know precisely what I was being shown. Again, I was reminded of excerpts from that ancient text. We'll discuss these in an upcoming chapter as well.

PART THREE

The third portion of the vision came, again, about one week later. It started with the very end of the prior vision with all the mud and people caught up in it at the bottom of the mountain, disappearing. My eyes were drawn up to the mountain and I saw it appearing exactly as the same mountain I did in the beginning of the second installment of the vision. It was devoid of anything on it and was that toffee-brown dirt color again.

Then unexpectedly, greenery of all types of foliage, plants, and trees began sprouting up all over the mountain. It was very much like watching time-lapse footage. When all the mountain was fully covered, I noticed that on different parts of the mountain, there were various types of foliage grouped together according to varying climates. My eyes were drawn in a bit closer, as if I kept clicking on a plus icon on a map to get closer, allowing me to see more and more elements. I saw meadows sprinkled with bright wildflowers gently swaying in a slight breeze, and pastures covered with the most plush, emerald green grass, looking so soft, I imagined it would be like walking barefoot on the most luxurious of carpeting.

I identified many streams and rivers cascading down the mountainside in between many jungles, forests, meadows, and fields. At that moment, my eyes were drawn to the exact center of the mountain. There was a very large river flowing, much wider than the others I was previously shown and it started at the very top of the mountain. It had beautiful trees with large leaves planted all along both sides and were laden with all kinds of fruit in a variety of vivid, mouthwatering colors. My eyes were then drawn to the visible root systems of these trees and they all had the very most outward tips in the river drinking up the water of the river.

Next, my eyes were drawn in closer and further down to the bottom of the trees where I saw a flurry of activity. Beneath these trees were people of all types, individuals of all ages, and from all walks of life. They looked weary and disheveled. Some then began to eat of the various types of fruit and before my very eyes, they were transformed. It looked like their clothing had been laundered and pressed. They now appeared fresh and energized. Then my eyes focused on one woman, in particular. She bit into a leaf she had plucked from a branch of the tree and got a look of pure joy on her face. She began to touch her forehead, cheeks, and neck. She lifted up her arms and surveyed them. Suddenly, she began to pull more leaves from the tree and drop them into an apron pocket. As she did so, I was able to somehow see into her mind, and I saw images of different people's faces flash across her forehead. I then just instantaneously knew she was thinking of others who she wanted to share these leaves with. With that, the vision ended. Once more, I was reminded of several corresponding prophecies and other text from that sacred book of ancient writings I own and cherish. I'll also share these with you in an upcoming chapter.

PART FOUR

Once more, approximately a week later, another segment of the vision came to me. This time, it started at the point of the time-lapse greenery growing and covering the entire mountain. My attention was shifted to the right of the large river flowing down the center of it. Suddenly, it felt as though I was free-falling and getting smaller as I fell. I abruptly came to a halt and found myself standing at street level. As I looked around at the homes that lined both sides of the street, I believed the era to be about the 1800s. As I was taking in the scenery, a woman in a light blue long hoop dress, full from her small waist down, with lace adorning the close-fitting top of the dress, walked by me and up the street. As I watched her, I noted that she had no idea of my existence and then I began taking in more detail. I observed that her hair was pinned up high on her head with one elegant banana curl adorning one side, and that she was holding up a matching parasol over herself. It was as though she appeared to confirm the time period I was estimating.

As I was pondering over this, my eyes were drawn to a street lamp on the edge of the sidewalk on the left side of the road. I was noticing that it was black and looked old fashioned when suddenly, dusk fell. And when dusk fell, the lamp lit up and it was then that I observed that it was an oil lamp, not an electric street light with an incandescent bulb. At this point, the vision ended. I thought about the vision several times as days passed and the one thing that was most profound to me, the one thing that really stuck with me, was that oil lamp.

It was a couple of weeks later when I was shown the vision again. Well, sort of. It was the same street and oil lamp but the scenery had changed to a different era. I once again saw a lady walking down the street. But this time the lady was walking a cute little dog on a red leash down the road. However, her clothing identified the time period to be that of the 1960s. I somehow just knew this was shown to me so I would understand that the exact era or time period was not the only thing of importance here, but also that the content of the vision was an ongoing truth, something that the Ancient of Days has been bringing forth over time. Once that revelation was acknowledged, my attention was drawn down onto the road by the sidewalk. It was as if I was supposed to perceive what season it was, because that also was of great significance here. I detected that it was very damp as the sidewalk and road were wet. My eyes shifted back to the sidewalk and edge of the road. Upon them were fallen leaves in varying shades of reds, yellows, and oranges. So, I looked up to the trees lining the sidewalk and road, and indeed, all of the leaves had changed into their fall colors.

My vision was drawn downward again and as I perused the sidewalk, my gaze following the scattered colorful leaves, I, again, identified the street-side oil lamp. I somehow just knew that it was of great importance as well. At this point, dusk fell afresh, and the oil lamp lit up. As I was intensely focused on the glowing light, it suddenly burned considerably brighter. Thinking it was getting darker, further into night, I looked up to the skies. To my amazement, it was not any darker at all. My eyes darted back to the oil streetlamp and what I observed was the light burned brighter because there was an increase in the amount of oil in it, and most assuredly not because night had fallen. Once my brain recognized the truth of this, the vision ended. I again was reminded of text from the sacred book of ancient writings, as well as some symbolic imagery contained within it. They have been sprinkled throughout these visions as I described them to you and we'll delve into them in upcoming chapters. But first we'll do some exploration as to why we are drawn to visions, dreams, prophecies, and other aspects of the intangible.

CHAPTER TWO

THE ETERNAL

Deep down, people have always known that there is something out there greater than themselves and greater than what the eye can see. They've felt it and it's hard to put down into words what that is exactly, because they just don't know, but they sense it. Therefore, some have been drawn to the possibility that there is life on other planets with beings of superior intellect than human beings, or that there is a spiritual realm out there and if they seek long enough, if they pursue it hard enough, they'll find it and become an enlightened being themselves. Or they've been drawn to clairvoyants, or mediums, or palm readers who seem to have tapped into a greater power. Or they've wondered about secret societies who claim to know the mysteries of the universe and its secrets. Or they even believe the universe is god or that there are a thousand different gods to choose from and we each get to choose which one we'll follow but will all end up in the same place.

Or perhaps they believe, no, the know that there are pure evil beings that live in the spiritual realm. Or because they've searched all or some of the above and came up unsatisfied, they've determined within themselves that there really isn't anything more to our existence other than the here and now, only what can be seen with the naked eyes, so therefore, let's eat, drink, and be merry and experience and enjoy every pleasure out there before we breathe our last breath and slip into nothingness, gone forever. And that is the key word – forever, also referred to as eternal. In essence, we all are searching for satisfaction and the choices, the roads that lead to it, can be found in abundance but never quite completely satisfy. And all of the various roads, all except one of them that is, lead to eternal destruction.

At this point, if you haven't figured it out yet, I should tell you that the ancient sacred text I refer to is the HOLY BIBLE and the Ancient of Days is God Almighty and His Son, the Lord Jesus

Christ, and not from some secret book written by the likes of Edgar Cayce, Nostradamus, or even from the old Mayan Calendar. Nor any other well-known or unknown medium or psychic or underground secret society, for that matter. They're not from old writings dug up in an archeological dig out in the middle of the desert. Nope, not even an old book on dream interpretations.

Wait! Before you slam the book shut and toss it aside in disappointment or disgust, please bear with me and hear me out. If you want nothing to do with the Bible, God, and Jesus, I'm going to assume it is because you've had negative experiences with people who claim to be Christians and/or people in "the church." I understand. I've been there. It's painful, creates emotional wounds, it hurts the heart, and leaves a sour taste in your mouth. You don't want nor need anything like that in your life. You know people "of the world" who are more loving, caring, understanding, and accepting than "those people," than "church people." I completely comprehend, but those people do not represent nor can compare to just one little touch from the Holy Spirit of God or His only begotten Son, Jesus, encompassing you with His presence and His pure love. I say this from personal experience, and can guarantee you that it far outweighs any harm or damage "those people" inflicted upon you.

As a matter of fact, my first negative experience with them occurred the very first time I went to church, that I can recall anyway, when I was a very young and impressionable little girl. I don't know how old I was, but I hadn't started school yet, so I was under the age of five. It was Easter Sunday and we were going to go to my grandmother's church, the church my mom attended school at through the eighth grade. I had on my new Easter dress, bonnet, and shoes, and was very excited. Once we were seated, I began to take in the scenery. All along the sides of church, there were beautiful colored stain glass windows. At the front, I spotted these magnificent white marble statues, then gold-colored vases with some of them holding beautiful greenery and leaves that looked like palm fronds and smaller vases holding yellow and white lilies. There was an older man with white hair dressed in a pristine white robe down to his feet. The robe had gold embroidery along the sleeves, hem, and front. Upon his head was a white beanie.

After people stood up and hymns that I did not know were sung, accompanied by a huge pipe organ, every one sat back down and the white robed man began to speak. Then suddenly, people in the pews began saying all the same thing, at the same time, sometimes with and sometimes in between the white-robed man's words. Sometimes they stood up when they spoke and at other times they didn't. Being the inquisitive little thing that I was, I began asking questions. I wanted to know how all the people knew to stand up at certain times. I was answered with, "Shhh!" I wanted to know how the people knew how to say the same thing at exactly the same time too, asking a bit louder this time. I did not like to be shushed. But I was met with another, "Shhh!"

I didn't like being ignored either, so I then tugged on my mom's dress sleeve, and whined rather loudly, "Mommy!" Just then, I felt my arm being grabbed. I looked over and saw a long skinny hand and fingers clutching, squeezing, and pulling on my arm. I was frightened because that skinny, boney hand looked just like the feet of the pheasants my dad hunted. As I looked up to the person yanking on me, my terror increased tenfold. There was a stooped old lady, so old, that the skin on her face was nothing but wrinkles and peering out from them were two sunken in dark beady-eyes. She was hunched over and was dressed in a black robe with a white collar and had on a black hood over her head. I started screaming and crying at this point, as she wrenched me up out of the pew and began dragging me toward the back of the church. I was calling out for my mom, but she didn't come rescue me. I was so frightened! As a matter of fact, not one single person in the pews seemed to even care, intensifying my terror.

Next, the scary lady was leading me up a winding, circular staircase that was all composed of fieldstone including the walls and the stairs themselves. When we reached the top, she led me through a door that led to a big room. Inside the dark, dank room, on the right-hand side, there was a glass window that took up over the top half of the whole wall. I kept crying out that I wanted my mommy in between sobs. Then the black-robed lady led me to that window and told me to look out and I could see my family. When I looked out, I noticed we were way up high and I could see all the people sitting in the pews. My eyes frantically searched for my grandma, mom, dad, sister, and brother. Once I spotted them, I cried even louder that I wanted my mommy. The creepy old lady told me that no one could hear me because I was in the "cry room" and it was sound proof. This frightened me even more, and I began to pound on the window with my little fists hoping to grab my family's attention. Creepy lady didn't like it and told me to shush and stop that pounding. I didn't listen to her because I was completely petrified!

Suddenly, I heard a loud crack while simultaneously feeling a whack across the back of my legs that left them stinging. As I turned around, I saw that scary old woman with a yardstick in her hand. She had struck me which only intensified my fear and my screams. She then grabbed my arm again and pointed to a brownish-red leather covered bench up against the wall and a cardboard box full of old toys. She told me to choose a toy to play with then sit down on that bench and play quietly. I was in no mood to play, so I made my way to the bench trying to quench my sobs. It took a lot of effort to make them subside. I sat down still shaking, sniffling, and wiping away my tears with the back of my hand. I winced every time a sob escaped although trying to keep them inside in fear of what that frightening old lady would do to me next. She pointed to the box of toys with a long, skinny, claw-like finger and told me to go get a toy. I shook my head no. She tried coaxing me to do it telling me all the children who came there loved to play with the toys. I still resisted. I did not feel like playing at all!

She hobbled over to the old cardboard toybox, reached in, and pulled out a scruffy looking doll. She then shuffled over to me and thrust that doll in my lap, commanding me to play. I looked down at that doll in my lap and saw she wore a dingy, faded, light pink dress. The doll's face was splotchy with smudges of dirt from days gone by and had closed eyes with thick, dark eyelashes. On the top of her head, were little plugs of what once was blonde hair but now looked like prickly bristles coming out of little holes in between dirty flesh colored rubber. I didn't want to touch her. She looked almost as creepy as the scary old woman. But she commanded me to play again, so I reluctantly did so. However, when I picked that doll up from my lap, right before my face, her eyes suddenly opened. Bink! The last thing I remember is chilling blue eyes staring at me, dropping the doll in fear, and letting out an ear-piercing scream. I honestly don't remember what happened next. I must have blocked it from my memory due to trauma. I mean, this was the stuff nightmares are made of!

As an adult, I wondered why my mom didn't stop the old woman from taking me. I remembered when she told me that she had attended school at that church until she entered high school. She shared with me her own horror story, of sorts, with nuns. She explained that she was born lefthanded, so she naturally held her pencil in her left hand. But the nuns would then whack the knuckles of her left hand with a ruler and make her put her pencil in her right hand, telling her she had to learn to write with her right hand. They said writing with your left hand was evil! I was flabbergasted! The only thing I can think of where that mindset came from, was perhaps when Jesus was sharing that during the final judgement, the Son of Man will separate people like a shepherd separates sheep from goats with the sheep on His right and the goats on His left. How that equates to being lefthanded as evil is beyond my comprehension and indeed, makes no sense. God created everything including right and left, as well as both righthanded and lefthanded people and He created them all in His own image. Anyway, I figure my mom was still intimidated by those nuns, and perhaps that particular old nun she may have recognized as one that actually did the whacking, so she consequently allowed her to take me. So, how is that for a bad experience with "church people"?

Let's now fast forward to when I was a young teenager, a mere thirteen years old. At the church I was being brought up in, a Pentecostal church, there was a girl, whom I'll refer to as Jan, who was my same age. She was in actuality, our pastor's wife's niece. Her mom was the pastor's wife's sister. Anyway, she and her mom invited me to go up north for the weekend. Jan's grandmother lived in Traverse City, and it was the time of the Cherry Festival. My parents consented and so I went with her, looking forward to having a positively fun time. When we were dropped off at Jan's grandmother's house, it was rather late, so we took showers and changed into our jammies and went straight to bed. Jan and I discussed what we would do the next day before drifting off to sleep.

We were up and ready early the next morning, and set out walking, excited to go to the fairgrounds and watch the tractor pulls and horse shows with the riders doing tricks. When we reached the fairgrounds, we chose to sit on the grass rather than cross to the other side to go to the bleachers. Because the ground was still dewy, my jeans got wet and subsequently muddy. Also, as the events took place, dust flew up and the breeze sometimes carried the clouds of dust right to us. By the time the events were over, the sun was higher and I was not only hot and sweaty, but dirty. I couldn't wait to get back to the house to clean up and change, while hearing in my mind, my adoptive mom telling me I could not wear certain clothes in public because they were old, dingy, and not suitable. She insisted that I must always be presentable in public and I assumed it was because if I wasn't clean and crisp, she would be embarrassed, thinking it was a reflection on her as a mom. Anyway, when we returned, I changed into a clean pair of shorts and exchanged my dirty sweatshirt for a tank top more suitable for the warmer temperature, after sponge bathing myself.

As afternoon approached, Jan asked her grandmother if we could walk uptown for the street dance that evening. Her grandmother gave us permission and said we could leave after supper. We ate outside at the picnic table that evening and I really don't remember what we ate except for dessert. It was the first time I had ever had cantaloupe and I absolutely loved my large slice with a scoop of vanilla ice cream on top. After supper, Jan and I went upstairs to get ready to go uptown. As she was brushing her hair, I changed into a clean pair of jeans and a thin long-sleeved blouse knowing it would cool down after the sun set. When we came back downstairs, Jan's grandmother looked at me and told me I was a hussy! Mind you, I didn't know what the word meant but could tell it wasn't anything good by the way she spat the word out. She then continued saying that I had changed clothes again and was wearing a third outfit that day only because I wanted to attract boys. I then understood the gist of the word, but, Eww! At that age, my thoughts about boys were that they were to be admired and crushed on from afar, not to be up close and personal, to hold hands or anything else! I couldn't believe she said that to me. She continued with her ranting, saying something about the moon turning red and Jesus returning to gather up His people which would not include hussies! Wow! As I continued to follow Jesus and Father God, there were many more negative and hurtful incidents in my life with "church people," but I'm confident I've made my point with those two above incidents.

As you can clearly see, I completely understand about "church people" and am thankful God sent true, loving Christians into my life who portrayed the love of Christ and who drew me to them via that Godly love, overshadowing the nasty, hurtful, and judgmental effects of "religious people" and hypocrites. Also, that He appeared to me personally when I cried out to Him when I had reached the end of myself. Please, also take comfort in the fact that Jesus Himself, the greatest teacher and prophet that ever lived, experienced the same thing. The "church people," the "religious people" of His day, were the religious leaders known as the Pharisees and Sadducees, and it didn't turn out so well for them!

Now, let's get back to the eternal and why we know there is something more out there, something more than the eye can see. The Bible teaches that humans are created with a longing to know God and teaches that the desire to know God is in fact, integral in humanity. In Ecclesiastes 3:10-11, we read – I have seen the God-given task with which the sons of men are to be occupied. He has made everything beautiful in its time. Also, He has put eternity in their hearts… God Himself has set the sense of eternity in our hearts. This means we were created with a built-in compass guiding us toward hope and greatness beyond the earthly, natural realm. It's an invitation for seekers to distinguish that life doesn't conclude with death; rather, our journey continues as part of God's eternal plan.

Let's look at some more Scriptures that compliment and expand on this fact. Psalm 107:9 – For He satisfies the longing soul, and fills the hungry soul with goodness. Proverbs 8:17 – I love those who love Me, And those who seek Me diligently will find Me. Jeremiah 29:13 – And you will seek Me and find Me, when You search for Me with all your heart. Lamentations 3:25 – The Lord is good to those who wait for Him, To the soul who seeks Him. And John 17:3 – And this is eternal life, that they may know You, the only true God, and Jesus Christ whom You have sent.

The verses above help us to understand our desire to seek the eternal and illustrate that knowing God is not just a choice, but a deep-seated yearning within us, reflecting our spiritual nature that God Himself created us with and chose us to be His, before the foundation of the earth was laid. And that those who seek Him will find Him because of that and be led into a personal, eternal relationship with Him through Jesus, and only then, will man find satisfaction for his soul. Proverbs 27:20 NLT says – Just as Death and Destruction are never satisfied, so human desire is never satisfied. – Our carnal being is never satisfied, but through the Lord alone, we find that satisfaction.

CHAPTER THREE

INTERPRETATION DO'S AND DON'TS

Before we get into the interpretation of the visions given from the Ancient of Days, we must first understand some vital truths concerning the Bible itself, Scripture interpretation, and many mistakes made while trying to interpret prophecy within and outside of the Holy Bible. First and foremost, the Bible is the very word of God. Scripture teaches us in 2 Timothy 3:16-17 – All Scripture is given by inspiration of God, and is profitable for doctrine, for reproof, for correction, for instruction in righteousness, that the man of God may be complete, thoroughly equipped for every good work.

It is revealed in John 1:1-5,14 – In the beginning was the Word, and the Word was with God, and the Word was God. He was in the beginning with God. All things were made through Him, and without Him nothing was made that was made. In Him was life, and the life was the light of men. And the light shines in the darkness, and the darkness did not comprehend it. And the Word became flesh and dwelt among us, and we beheld His glory, the glory as of the only begotten of the Father, full of grace and truth.

It tells us in 2 Peter 1:19-21 – And so we have the prophetic word confirmed, which you do well to heed as a light that shines in a dark place, until the day dawns and the morning star rises in your hearts; knowing this first, that no prophecy of Scripture is of any private interpretation, for prophecy never came by the will of man, but holy men of God spoke as they were moved by the Holy Spirit.

What we learn through these Scripture passages is that all Scripture is God breathed – God inspired, that the Word is Jesus and was with God from the very beginning. We also learn that the Scriptures were written by human men, yes, but inspired by God through His Holy Spirit. The whole Godhead is revealed in the above Scripture passages; God the Father, God the Son, and God the Holy Spirit. We are also taught that the Word is of no private interpretation, in other words, we humans cannot interpret it to mean what we think it might mean or what we want it to mean. It means what God reveals it means and therefore, in essence, the whole Bible is prophetic. And to give us further clarification on that, He also has given us Numbers 23:19 – "God is not a man, that He should lie, nor a son of man, that He should repent. Has He said, and will not He do? Or has He spoken and will He not make it good? We can couple that with 2 Corinthians 1:31 where Paul says, "By the mouth of two or three witnesses every word shall be established." And you can rest assured that God has established His Word.

For instance, Bible scholars estimate that there are well over 63,000 cross references of Scripture throughout the Bible. If that number alone doesn't intrigue or impress you, then how about this? That number of cross references is more than the number of verses in the entire Bible itself. Scholars estimate there to be approximately 31,102 verses and this, of course, depends on which translation and version you use. And if that isn't incredible enough for you, how about these stats? The Bible was written over a span of 1500 years, by over 40 different authors, on three different continents, and in three different languages, and yet, it reads as one congruent, unified message.

This proves that mere men did not write the Bible, but these men were inspired by the Holy Spirit moving upon them to write what was written. It also reiterates that Scripture or the Bible interprets itself, and any mere man should not do the interpreting on his own. The Bible does touch on this in Acts 17:11 when Paul visited Berea. – "These (the Bereans) were more fair-minded…in that they received the word with all readiness, and searched the Scriptures daily to find out whether these things were true." And that is what we all must do so as not to be deceived and we should do it via prayer and with the guidance of the Holy Spirit in making the Scriptures alive to us, giving us understanding and revelation. The Bereans' example should serve as a model for us in approaching teachings, doctrine, and prophecy – by investigating the Scriptures, then confirming that truth from other Scriptures.

We must be diligent in doing what the Bereans did because it is all too easy to follow the ideas of men. When Jesus was explaining to His followers about end time events, He said to them in Matthew 24:4 – "Take heed that no one deceives you." Throughout history and ongoing today, there are numerous people who have taught and are teaching their own ideas about what Bible prophecy says, and therefore, there are a myriad of false teachers and prophets in the world. Scripture tells us 1 Thessalonians 5:20-21 – "Do not quench the Spirit. Do not despise prophecies. Test all things; hold fast what is good." Unfortunately, it is way too easy to just believe whatever makes sense in our own minds when we first hear it. But Proverbs 3:5-7 instructs us – "Trust in the Lord with all of your heart, and lean not to your own understanding; In all your ways acknowledge Him, and He shall direct your paths. Do not be wise in your own eyes; Fear the Lord and depart from evil."

Also, it's so easy to search the Scriptures to find one that reiterates what we already believe, what we already have a preconceived notion about, whether it's abortion, alcohol, baptism, divorce, homosexuality, speaking in tongues, etc. and even the meaning of prophecy and whether it should be continuing in the days we live in. If we're just searching the Scriptures to reinforce, in our own mind, something we already believe, we will surely find it! But as we've already discussed, that's the incorrect way, for we'll only end up strengthening our own self-deception. One more common sorrowful mistake is allowing the Holy Spirit to reveal the truth of Bible prophecy and Scripture to us, but because we want to fit in with the crowd, or perhaps people please, we are more concerned about what other people will think of us and don't live according to those truths. The Holy Scriptures, in fact, address this in John 12:42-43 – "Nevertheless even among the rulers many believed in Him, but because of the Pharisees they did not confess Him, lest they should be put out of the synagogue; for they loved the praise of men more than the praise of God." And Romans 10:9 states emphatically – For with the heart one believes unto righteousness, and with the mouth confession is made onto salvation.

Another thing we must understand regarding prophecy are the purposes of it. In Ezekiel 33:1-9, we find that God spoke to the prophet Ezekiel telling him that God had called him to be a watchman on the wall. And when God gave him a warning for the people, he was to then warn them. If the people didn't heed the prophet's words, their blood would be upon their own hands and not the prophet's, however, if the prophet failed to warn the people, then their blood would be upon the prophet's hands. This is just one reason we are not to despise prophecies, but rather to test them, to see if they line up with the Bible and if they do, respond correctly. Don't be just a gatherer of prophetic information to be in the know, but rather, heed what the prophecies are revealing, and make personal adjustments if needed.

An additional vital aspect of prophecy in the Scriptures, is that often prophecies come to pass short term, to a degree, with a much deeper fulfillment long term, at a later time, as well as far into the future. Let's examine one example of this. Joel, after speaking of "the day of the Lord" then proclaims prophetically in chapter 2, verses 28-29 – "And it shall come to pass afterward that I will pour out My Spirit on all flesh; your sons and your daughters shall prophesy, your old men shall dream dreams, your young men shall see visions. And also on My menservants and on My maidservants, I will pour out My Spirit in those days."

This came to pass short term in the Book of Acts on the day of Pentecost. Peter pronounces this in Acts 2:14-18 – But Peter, standing up with the eleven, raised his voice and said to them, Men of Judea and all who dwell in Jerusalem, let this be known to you, and heed my words. For these are not drunk, as you suppose, since it is only the third hour of the day. But this is what was spoken by the prophet Joel: "And it shall come to pass in the last days, says God, That I will pour out of My Spirit on all flesh; your sons and your daughters shall prophesy, your young men shall see visions, your old men shall dream dreams. And on My menservants and on My maidservants, I will pour out My Spirit in those days; and they shall prophesy." And this is exactly what happened when the disciples were all gathered together in one accord praying as Jesus had instructed them to do. Suddenly, the Holy Spirit appeared as a flame over them all individually, and they began praying in the Spirit, in tongues that were not their native language, and the people from many different regions understood in their own native language what was being declared. The crowd of people either didn't understand what was happening or thought the twelve were drunk. (Acts 2:1-13) This surely is classified as a miraculous wonder in the earth.

However, this was only a partial fulfillment of Joel's prophecy, for the rest of it found in Joel 2:30 speaks of blood and fire and pillars of smoke. It also declares, in verse 31, that the sun shall be turned into darkness, and the moon into blood, before the coming of the great and awesome day of the Lord, and of the gathering of the nations for judgement in Chapter 3, verses 1-2. Obviously, that hasn't occurred yet, and speaks to the future when Jesus returns. This is also spoke of in the Book of Revelation, chapter 16:14-16. – For they are spirits of demons, performing signs, which go out to the kings of the earth and of the whole world, to gather them to the battle of that great day of God Almighty. Next Jesus says in verse 15, "Behold, I am coming as a thief. Blessed is he who watches, and keeps his garments, lest he walk naked and they see his shame." Continuing in verse 16 – And they gathered them together to the place in Hebrew, Armageddon. – At this time, God's enemies will most assuredly experience that great and awesome day of the Lord!

If you think of the time span involved in this prophecy as well as others that have more than one fulfillment, it's just mindboggling! God is amazing! How does He do it? Isaiah 46:9-10 NLT gives us His answer. – "Remember the things I have done in the past. For I alone am God, and there is none like Me. Only I can tell you the future before it happens. Everything I plan will come to pass, for I do whatever I wish." And in Daniel 2:20-22 NLT, Daniel declares "Praise the name of God forever and ever, for He has all wisdom and power. He controls the course of world events; he removes kings and sets up other kings. He gives wisdom to the wise and knowledge to the scholar. He reveals deep and mysterious things and knows what lies hidden in darkness, though He is surrounded by light." Hallelujah! Praise His holy name!

Next, let's look at some examples of what happened when mere men tried to interpret the Word and prophecies within it, out of their own natural understanding, and void of the Holy Spirit's inspiration and revelation, coupled with not checking it with other Scripture. Especially with Matthew 24:35-36 – "Heaven and earth will pass away, but My words will by no means pass away. But of that day and hour no one knows, not even the angels of heaven, but My Father only." And that has caused many obvious misinterpretations that are replayed repeatedly, with various reasonings behind it; that being Jesus' return and the end of the world. Believe it or not, these false predictions span from the first to the twenty-first century! Let's touch on a just a few of them. We find some examples of this in the New Testament. One such example is found in 2 Thessalonians 2:1-2 "Now, brethren, concerning the coming of our Lord Jesus Christ and our gathering together to Him, we ask you, not to be soon shaken in mind or by word or by letter, as if from us, as though the Day of Christ had come." Here Paul warned the Thessalonians around AD 50 not to be shaken up or distressed if they hear that the day of the Lord had already come, and then gives them some other things that must happen first, before that day.

Another example is the year 1666. Many took the year 1,000 (the millennium) combined it with 666 (the mark of the beast) and theorized that 1666 marked the end of the world. Interestingly enough, in 1666, the Bubonic plague had broken out in London and was ongoing in that year and also the Great London Fire followed, but the world did not end. A Quaker by the name of George Fox wrote that every single thunderstorm in that year provoked suspicion and expectation of the end of time. Also, in 1789, many English Bible interpreters thought the French Revolution was the unfolding of the prophecies of Daniel chapter 7 and Revelation 13, right before their very eyes. More recent historical predictions came from Edgar C. Whisenant who wrote a book "88 Reasons Why the Rapture Will Be in 1988" and sold over two million copies! Within it, he predicted the day as being in September, between the 11th and 13th of 1988. What is just astounding to me, is that he did indeed know Matthew 24:36, however, he brushed it aside reasoning that we can't know the day or hour, but we can know the month and year! Yikes! Even more incredulous, is that in the year 1989, he wrote another book titled "The Final Shout: Rapture Report 1989. What went wrong in 1988" Inside, he explained all his miscalculations getting to 1988, but now knew it would be 1989. To me, that is just incredulous!

There was another recent prediction made, but for the year 1994 by the president of Family Radio, Harold Camping. He wrote a book called "1994?" as well as a sequel titled "Are You Ready?" Within, he used his own very complicated, totally unorthodox, method of dating, numerology, and allegory pointing to Jesus' return occurring in September of 1994. Even after the date had passed and everyone was still here, he still was convinced that Jesus was coming back very soon. And even in 2025 another prediction was made by a South African Pastor, Joshua Mhlakela, as well as some others, for September 23-24 based upon a vision he said was given to him and coupled with the Jewish holiday Rosh Hashanah. But the date came and went, uneventfully.

There are also some upcoming dates predicting the return of Jesus. But the most interesting one to me, is the prediction of 2060 made by Isaac Newton. He's known for his interest in Biblical prophecy, for believing science and the Scriptures complement each other, and believed a new era would be ushered in, in the year 2060, rather than an actual apocalypse as others have believed and predicted. He also is known to have reservations about predicting actual dates of the end of the world, fearing that predictions such as those would cause people to discredit the Scriptures he so loved. Regardless, the other above accounts are great reasons to know the Word of God and be led by His Holy Spirit in understanding it, for mere men cannot put God on their own timeline. Only God Almighty alone knows when all His plans and purposes will come to fruition and be fulfilled.

Jesus spoke to the religious sect of His time in regards to this as well. Matthew 16:1-2. "When it is evening you say, 'It will be fair weather, for the sky is red;' and in the morning, 'It will be foul weather today, for the sky is red and threatening.' Hypocrites! You know how to discern the face of the sky, but you cannot discern the signs of the times." As well as multitudes of people in Luke 12:54-56, Then He said to the multitudes, "Whenever you see a cloud rising out of the west, immediately you say, 'A shower is coming';

and so it is. And when you see the south wind blow, you say, 'There will be hot weather;' and there is. Hypocrites! You can discern the face of the sky and of the earth. But how is it you do not discern this time?" In these passages, Jesus is declaring to the people that they are able to understand natural signs and predict weather changes based on the sky, and He also criticizes them for not being able to recognize deeper Spiritual truths and prophetic signs of their times, especially the significance of His ministry in their day. For the Law, Psalms, and Prophets all spoke of His coming and they studied these intensely.

Also, while in prayer, the Spirit of the Lord revealed another reason why so many have made false predictions and even wrote books with false narratives of His Word. Remember, not too long ago, a whole book series was written about the end times, the antichrist, the beast, etc. and the Book of Revelation. It falsely depicted the people of God, Christians, as barely holding on, frightened of the power of evil that would surely overtake them if Jesus didn't come back quickly and rescue his cowering, fearful people in hiding, just in the nick of time. Ha! The authors of that series must not have read or perhaps just ignored other Scripture and other parts of the Book of Revelation that say quite clearly, that His people will be victorious and overcomers. Let's look at a few verses in Revelation where Jesus proclaims this. Rev. 2:7…To him who overcomes I will give to eat from the tree of life… Rev. 2:11…He who overcomes shall not be hurt by the second death. Rev.2:26 – And he who overcomes, and keeps My works until the end, to him I will give power over the nations. Rev. 3:5 – He who overcomes shall be clothed in white garments, and I will not blot out his name from the Book of Life; but I will confess his name before My Father and before His angels.

Other Scripture along the same lines is in Matthew 16:19 where Jesus declares He is building His Church and the gates of Hell will not prevail against it. That declaration clearly states that despite challenges, the church will most assuredly prevail against dark forces! And in Ephesians 5:27 it undeniably affirms that Jesus loves the church and is working to present her to Himself as a glorious bride/church without spot or wrinkle, Holy and acceptable, not feeble and trembling.

Now, let's read my favorites from Revelation. Revelation 12:10-11– Then I heard a loud voice saying in heaven, "Now salvation, and strength, and the kingdom of our God, and the power of His Christ have come, for the accuser of our brethren, who accused them before our God day and night, has been cast down. And they overcame him by the blood of the Lamb and by the word of their testimony, and did not love their lives to the death." Revelation 19:11-15 – Now, I saw heaven opened, and behold, a white horse. And He who sat on him was called Faithful and True, and in righteousness He judges and makes war. His eyes were like a flame of fire, and on His head were many crowns. He had a name written that no one knew except Himself. He was clothed with a robe dipped in blood, and His name is called The Word of God. And the armies in heaven, clothed in fine linen, white and clean, followed Him on white horses. (that's us, the saints of God, victorious overcomers) Now out of His mouth goes a sharp sword, that with it He should strike the nations. And He Himself will rule them with a rod of iron. He himself treads the winepress of the fierceness and wrath of Almighty God. See? They forgot those parts of the Bible. There will be no fear filled church weak and cowering and in hiding at His return!

Next, let's look at some more Scripture that strengthens why we must be able, through the Holy Spirit, to discern both the natural times together with God's Spiritual times, and ask Him for wisdom regarding them. Hosea 14:9 – Who is wise? Let him understand those things. Who is prudent? Let him know them. For the ways of the Lord are right; the righteous walk in them, but the transgressors stumble in them. Proverbs 17:24 – Wisdom is in the sight of him who has understanding, but the eyes of a fool are on the ends of the earth. And finally, let's read what 2 Timothy 3:1-4,7 declares – But know this, that in the last days perilous times will come: For men will be lovers of themselves, lovers of money, boasters, proud, blasphemers, disobedient to parents, unthankful, unholy, unloving, unforgiving, slanderers, without self-control, brutal, despisers of good, traitors, headstrong, haughty, lovers of pleasure rather than lovers of God…always learning and never able to come to the truth.

After reading those verses in 2 Timothy, the Lord asked me for how many generations of my family has that Scripture passage been discussed and it was then that I knew what He was conveying. From listening to my grandparents, parents, and from what I've seen in my own life, every decade since the 1920s has witnessed what they referred to as the degradation of morals and behavior from the preceding decade, and therefore, Jesus' return will most likely occur quickly. This is what I personally know, but I'm quite confidant people have probably been saying this for centuries. The point is that people have been looking at what they see with their own eyes and with their own perception and understanding and proclaiming that Jesus is coming back quickly. However, they hadn't taken into account other Scripture that speaks of His return and other events that would be taking place before and simultaneously. In that sense, it was no different than those people Jesus was criticizing for making predictions from what they see in the natural only.

May we all pray and ask God for His Holy Spirit to give us revelation and wisdom concerning His Word and of the times we are living in now, a time of His visitation on the earth, akin to when Jesus visited them in their day. And for Spiritual wisdom and discernment in conjunction with the Scriptures, the written Word, to keep us from being deceived or misled. Thank you, Father, in Jesus' name!

CHAPTER FOUR

THE SNOWY MOUNTAIN

Before we get into the interpretation of the visions of mountain scenes the Lord gave me, I want to share with you that when I sat down to write them out, the Ancient of Days asked me to turn to the Book of Daniel, chapter 2 and read about King Nebuchadnezzar's dream. Not the interpretation of it given by Daniel, but when Daniel was relaying to the king what he actually saw happening in his dream. I immediately searched for it in my Bible and found what God was showing me when I read it. It is in verse 35…And the stone that struck the image became a great mountain and filled the whole earth. I instantly asked Him if He was revealing to me that His holy mountain was the whole earth. I did not receive a direct answer from Him, so I continued to ponder on it from time to time.

Let's now explore the meaning the Holy Spirit gave me concerning the first installment of the continuing vision. Recall how the first thing I saw was a mountain covered in snow. The Scriptures teach us that snow represents several things. First, let's look at Isaiah 55:10. It articulates God's sovereignty over the earth and His pronouncing snow as being seasonal. It reads in part – "For as the rain comes down and snow from heaven, and do not return there, but water the earth, and make it bring forth and bud…" Here, in speaking of the attributes of seasons, I understood that God was saying that we, on earth, have entered into a new season in Him.

Also, we learn in Job 37:6-13 – For He says to the snow, "Fall on the earth"; Likewise to the gentle rain and the heavy rain of His strength. He seals the hand of every man, that all men may know His work…By the breath of God ice is given, and the broad waters are frozen…He scatters His bright clouds and they swirl about, being turned by His guidance, that they may do whatever He commands them on the face of the whole earth. He causes it to come whether for correction, or for His land, or for mercy. – What we'll focus on now, is again, God is in charge of the seasons, and that He has a purpose for each season, so that man shall know His work, including the winter season. We'll reference the above verses again, a little bit later.

Snow also signifies an opportunity for renewal, speaks of purity, transformative power, cleansing, and the forgiveness of sins when we sincerely ask for it, therefore, this season that is upon us is a great opportunity for God's people to renew themselves in Him and for unredeemed mankind to come into Jesus' fold. Isaiah 1:18 declares – "Come now, and let us reason together," says the Lord, "Though your sins are like scarlet, they shall be as white as snow; though they are red like crimson, they shall be as wool." Here, God speaks of the cleansing of sin, forgiveness, and His ability to transform and renew us. In Psalm 51:7 the psalmist prays, "Purge me with hyssop, and I shall be clean; wash me, and I shall be whiter than snow." This verse speaks of spiritual renewal and of being made pure and renewed through God's mercy and grace. Daniel 7:9 reads, "I watched till thrones were put in place, and the Ancient of Days was seated: His garment was as white as snow and the hair of His head was like pure wool…" And Revelation 1:14 reveals, "His head and hair were white like wool, as white as snow…" In both Daniel's description of the Ancient of Days in the Book of Daniel, and John's description of Jesus resurrected in the Book of Revelation, snow is representative of and emphasizes divine purity, authority, wisdom, and the transformative power of Jesus Christ.

What happened next, is that my attention was drawn to the top of the mountain and that holds substantial meaning. Throughout the Scriptures we find that mountaintops are meeting places between God and men, where God visits the earth for divine purposes and therefore represents where heaven and earth meet. It's a reflective representation of God's desire to speak to and abide with His people, reveal His glory, make known to men their God-given purpose, and establish His Kingdom. A few examples are where God called Moses and met him on the mountain via a burning bush, Abraham's call to sacrifice his only son to God, Elijah's encounter and showdown on Mount Carmel, and Jesus' transfiguration before a select few disciples in the New Testament.

Once my attention was drawn to the mountaintop, I viewed skiers, snowmobilers, and hikers. When I sought the Lord as to what these meant, He instructed me to notice that they were all engaged in ordinary activities. Once He spoke that, I was reminded of the people in Noah's time. It was then that I experienced the powerful rumbling of the mountain in the vision and was shown the avalanche taking out one skier while the other miraculously rose above the powerful wave of snow, as well as one snowmobiler wondrously covered and protected under the wave of snow while the other was taken out by it. At this point, the Holy Spirit brought back to my remembrance that the children of Israel, after traversing through the desert, were visited by God atop Mount Sinai. In part, Exodus 19:18 discloses that God descended upon Mount Sinai and the whole mountain quaked greatly. This shaking and quaking of the mountain represented that not only are we living in a new season in Him, but are also experiencing a time of God's great visitation upon the earth. We are truly living in amazing times!

In getting back to the two skiers and snowmobilers, Jesus, as He sat on the Mount of Olives, after telling His disciples that no one knows the day or hour of the sign of His coming and the end of the age, except His Father, taught how it would be in that time in Matthew 24. In verses 37-39, He revealed, "But as the days of Noah were, so also will the coming of the Son of Man be. For as in the days before the flood they were eating and drinking, and marrying and giving in marriage, until the day that Noah entered the ark, and did not know until the flood came and took them all away, so also will the coming of the Son of Man be." In other words, the people were enjoying all the luxuries the world had to offer and were totally oblivious, or were willfully ignorant of what was coming even though we're told in 2 Peter 2:5 that God didn't spare the ancient world, but saved Noah, one of only eight people, a preacher of righteousness, bringing in the flood on the world of the ungodly. Theologians estimate it took Noah over 100 years to build the ark and because Noah is referred to as a preacher of righteousness above, those people had all that time to heed the warnings of impending judgement, but rather, chose to continue relishing the luxuries of the world and following their own desires. Jesus said that's how it would be at His coming. May that be a wake-up call to us all!

Continuing in Matthew 24, Jesus continued His discourse in verses 40-44 teaching, "Then two men will be in the field: one will be taken and the other left. Two women will be grinding at the mill: one will be taken and the other left. Watch therefore, for you do not know what hour your Lord is coming. But know this, that if the master of the house had known what hour the thief would come, he would have watched and not allowed his house to be broken into. Therefore you also be ready, for the Son of Man is coming at an hour you do not expect." This was what the one skier and snowmobiler remaining and one of each disappearing was representing.

At this point, the Ancient of Days spoke saying, "Judgement always comes with an invitation for mercy." I knew then, that He meant not the final judgement as Jesus describes in Matthew 25:31-46 "When the Son of Man comes in all of His glory, and all of the holy angels with Him, then He will sit on the throne of His glory. All the nations will be gathered before Him, and He will separate them one from another, as a shepherd divides his sheep from the goats. And He will set the sheep on His right hand, but the goats on the left. Then the King will say to those on His right hand, 'Come, you blessed of My Father, inherit the kingdom prepared for you from the foundation of the world…' Then He will also say to those on the left hand, 'Depart from Me, you cursed, into the everlasting fire prepared for the devil and his angels'…And these will go away into everlasting punishment, but the righteous into eternal life." So, therefore, He was speaking of a soft or short-term, present judgement.

Upon hearing the Lord speak this, I asked Him to show me in His written Word where we see this, and he first gave me Galatians 6:7 – Do not be deceived, God is not mocked; for whatever a man sows, that he will also reap. – This is a principle that God has set forth in the earth. New Agers refer to it as karma, and in colloquial or everyday common language, it's expressed as, "What goes around, comes around." Nevertheless, it is a principle that God set forth in the earth. He next gave me, from Luke 15:11-24, the story of the prodigal son. This son asks his father for his inheritance, what was due him, and was given it. The son went to a faraway country and proceeded to blow it all on prodigal or wasteful living. Right when he had squandered it all away, a famine hit in that country so the son joined himself to a citizen of that country who sent him to his pigs. As this prodigal son was feeding those pigs, he was so hungry he would have gladly eaten the pig food, if only someone would give him some.

At this time, the son wakes up, comes to his senses, and realizes that even the servants at his father's house have more than enough of food to eat and here he was languishing in hunger. He plans to return to his father's house, repent of his wrong doing against God and his father, ask for forgiveness, and request of his father to live at home again, however, as a servant, knowing he wasn't worthy enough to be called a son any longer. He then headed home. But when he was still a way off from home, his father spotted him and had compassion on him, ran out to him, and kissed his neck. The son said what he planned on saying to his father including that he wasn't even worthy to be called his son. But his father called out to his servants asking them to bring out the best robe and clothe his son in it, to put a ring on his finger, and sandals on his feet. He then ordered the fatted calf to be prepared for the son's return exclaiming, "For my son was dead and is alive again, he was lost but now is found." This is an example of reaping what you sow and an invitation of mercy. The son wasted his possessions and reaped from his actions, that of being destitute and living with pigs, longing for pig food. When he woke up, or in other words, came back to his senses, and realized this was a soft judgement that he had brought upon himself, he knew he needed to seek out his father, confessing he had sinned against God and his father. So, what happened then? His father bestowed mercy on him and celebrated his turning back.

I don't know if you've ever been to a farm and seen what pigs eat or not, but I can tell you that it's nasty, stinks, and is comprised of what we would refer to as garbage. Jesus tells us that He is the bread of life and John describes Him as the very Word of God. So, when we feast on the Scriptures, we are eating spiritual, heavenly food full of wisdom, filling ourselves with the Word of God. But if we don't, we are being fed the wisdom of the world which is foolishness to God, or in other words, worldly, spiritual slop, garbage. The Scriptures do tell us that if we confess our sins, then God is faithful and just, forgiving our sins and cleansing us from all unrighteousness. Let this be an encouragement to all of God's children who have gone astray that their Father God is calling them back home. And for those that haven't accepted Jesus as their Lord and Savior yet, to know that their heavenly Father is calling them home with the awaiting gift of salvation, forgiveness, and mercy!

Let's now return to 2 Peter 2 and pick up in verses 6-9 – and turning the cities of Sodom and Gomorrah into ashes, condemned them to destruction, making them an example to those who afterward would live ungodly; and delivered righteous Lot, who was oppressed by the filthy conduct of the wicked (for that righteous man, dwelling among them, tormented his righteous soul from day to day by seeing and hearing their lawless deeds) — then the Lord knows how to deliver the Godly out of temptation and to reserve the unjust under punishment for the day of judgment. This is another example of pending judgement and the invitation to mercy. God extended mercy to Lot who lived righteously among wickedness. Notice now, that God did offer mercy to all the wicked people in Noah's time too, via Noah's preaching all those years as he was building the ark, but they refused His mercy. Just like them, we also get to accept God's invitation for mercy, if we so choose. The choice is ours to make.

We learn of another aspect of God's judgement and mercy in James 2:12-13. It teaches, So speak and so do as those who will be judged by the law of liberty. For judgement is without mercy to the one who has shown no mercy. Mercy triumphs over judgement. Once again, we are reminded of the sowing and reaping principle mentioned earlier. Accountability of our actions goes hand in hand with judgement. It's a reminder that we be especially mindful of how we treat others as we live out our lives. God desires that we reflect

His nature of love, mercy, and grace to others as we have been given these same unmerited gifts from Him.

As we discussed earlier in this chapter, regarding the snowy mountain vision about God sending snow from the Book of Job, we learned that snow represents God sending the snow for correction, and for mercy, and to mark the hand of every man. May we understand this visitation of God and this season we're in, and adjust our course, if need be, remembering that judgement always comes with an invitation for mercy from our merciful God, through His only begotten Son, Jesus!

Lastly, we'll discuss the meaning of the ten mountain climbers. In the vision, after the avalanche swept down the mountainside, only five hikers remained. The hikers who had pick axes and backpacks fully loaded up with gear and other provisions, ready for whatever may happen during their expedition were the ones remaining, however, the hikers who only had the pick axes, were nowhere to be seen, no longer on God's Holy Mountain. This scene is reminiscent of the parable of the ten virgins found in Matthew 25, in continuation of Jesus revealing to His disciples what would happen at the end of the age and giving them signs of what to watch for when His return is nearing.

He then goes on to tell them a parable. Let's take a look at it. Verses 1-13 NLT – "Then the Kingdom of Heaven will be like ten bridesmaids who took their lamps and went to meet the bridegroom. Five of them were foolish and five of them were wise. The five who were foolish didn't take enough olive oil for their lamps, but the other five were wise enough to take along extra oil. When the bridegroom was delayed, they all became drowsy and fell asleep.

At midnight they were roused by the shout, 'Look, the bridegroom is coming! Come out and meet him!' All the bridesmaids got up and prepared their lamps. Then the five foolish ones asked the others, 'Please give us some of your oil because our lamps are going out.' But the others replied, 'We don't have enough for all of us. Go to a shop and buy some for yourselves.'

But while they were gone to buy oil, the bridegroom came. Then those who were ready went in with him to the marriage feast, and the door was locked. Later, when the other five bridesmaids returned, they stood outside, calling, 'Lord! Lord! Open the door for us!' But he called back, 'Believe me, I don't know you!' So you, too, must keep watch! For you do not know the day or hour of my return."

The reason I chose the NLT version to share this parable with you is because it reminded me of the marriage traditions of the Middle East once shared with me. When I worked for Dr. Sadik, she invited all the girls in the office over to her home for a Christmas party. While there, she was sharing the traditions of her home country with us, including their marriage ceremonies. She then told us she had a video of her marriage to her husband and we all begged her to show it to us, which she did. She then explained their wedding traditions with us after we all watched it. She relayed to us that in the Middle East, their festivities included that the bridegroom and his friends were to come to the bride's house or wherever the festivities were to be held.

The bride's close friends, her bridesmaids, (as opposed to virgins) were to light up the way with lamps for the bridegroom and his friends and lead or escort them to where the wedding banquet was to take place. They then would enter the wedding and celebrate with the bridegroom. So, the bridesmaids' job was to listen for the announcement of the bridegroom and his friends approaching. When they heard it, it was then that they were to trim their lamps, light them, and then go out, showing the way for the bridegroom and company. Dr. Sadik explained that many marriages were arranged by their parents and therefore many of the bridegrooms came from other towns and no one knew how long it would take them to arrive, especially not knowing what he might encounter on the way that could cause a delay, all of this causing a buildup of excitement, and encouraging everybody to be continually ready. Then the bride and bridegroom would be dressed up as a king and queen and would celebrate for a whole week.

What I find interesting, is the way Jesus presented the parable pointing to the fact that His coming would be a long way off. In verse 5 "When the bridegroom was delayed, they all fell asleep." We could definitely say that over 2000 years is a long wait and we can discern, in observing with a spiritual perspective, that the world today is spiritually dark right now. Next, notice all ten bridesmaids fell asleep while waiting in the dark. Although we have no idea as to how much darkness will actually cover the earth, we should know that we Christians are called to be light to those perishing in the darkness and show or illuminate the way for them to be transferred out of that darkness into Jesus' marvelous light. 2 Peter 3:3-4 teaches us – Knowing this first: that scoffers will come in the last days, walking according to their own lusts, and saying, "Where is the promise of His coming? For since the fathers fell asleep, all things continue as they were from the beginning of creation." And as we look out into society today, we see people scorning and ridiculing Christians for believing in what they call a "2000-year-old fairy tale". We also find that sadly, some churches today don't even teach about Jesus' coming for His victorious bride without spot nor wrinkle, at all.

Let's look at the ten bridesmaids in the parable again. All ten of them represent those who profess to be Christians, carrying His light, but we find that five really are not, they only carry a lamp, but not the oil for the light. Regrettably, there are many hypocrites out there, just as in Jesus' day, who profess God with their mouth, but their heart is far from Him. Proverbs 20:27 says," The spirit of a man is the lamp of the Lord, searching all the inner depths of the heart." And Jesus said in John 8:12 – "I am the light of the world. He who follows Me shall not walk in darkness, but have the light of life. May we be like the five wise bridesmaids who lit up the darkness carrying the light of Jesus, the Holy Spirit, within them because they were prepared for His possible ongoing delay.

Let us not be like the five foolish bridesmaids who weren't prepared, procrastinating at very important decisions, and falling asleep at the midnight hour, the darkest hour of the night. They therefore didn't have the oil, the Holy Spirit, residing within their hearts at the final call to the wedding feast, although they thought they did. In that hour, no one will be able share their oil with anyone else because the Scriptures say we are to work out our own soul's salvation with fear and trembling and that the day of salvation is today. The door will be shut on them forever for we have no promise of tomorrow. Another sad fact is these foolish bridesmaids also made the mistake of believing they could leave and go get the oil for their lamps and return to the wedding celebration a little later, but were met with a permanently shut and locked door, and the voice of the bridegroom telling them, "Believe me! I don't know you!" Sadly, they knew of Jesus, but didn't know Him personally, never asking Him to be the Lord of their lives, inviting Him in.

The Bible tells us in so many ways that Jesus is returning for His church, and those who are not included, due to poor choices or procrastination, won't be invited to the Marriage of the Lamb. For them, final judgement is certain. But praise His Holy name! He has declared that judgement never comes without an invitation to His mercy! Let those that have an ear, hear what the Holy Spirit of God is speaking, and accept God's mercy and Jesus' invitation to the wedding of the Lamb before time runs out! Amen!

CHAPTER FIVE

THE MUDDY MOUNTAIN

Recall in the second vision given me, the mountain was barren, devoid of anything on it, was the color of dirt, and reminded me of a volcano. What came next was a powerful sensation again and that intense shaking and vibrating, similar to the shaking in the first installment of the vision. We only touched a bit about mountains shaking representing a visitation from God to the earth in the prior chapter. Here, we're going to go more in depth to gain greater understanding.

First, we'll look at examples of God visiting the earth with literal shaking and then later, at the spiritual shakings as well. We've already discussed God meeting the Israelites at Mount Sinai and the whole mountain shaking and quaking upon His visitation in the last chapter. Other examples in the Scriptures include Jeremiah 4:24 – I beheld the mountains, and indeed they trembled, and all the hills moved back and forth, and Habakuk 3:10 – "The mountains saw You and trembled..." Nahum 1:5 – "The mountains quake before Him, The hills melt, And the earth heaves at His presence, Yes, the world and all in it." We also have Psalm 97:5 – "The mountains melt like wax at the presence of the LORD, at the presence of the Lord of the whole earth." Psalm 18:7 – Then the earth shook and trembled; The foundations of the hills also quaked and were shaken Because He was angry. And back to Exodus, Exodus 19:18 – "Now Mount Sinai was completely in smoke, because the Lord descended upon it in fire. Its smoke ascended like the smoke of a furnace, and the whole mountain quaked greatly." The above Scripture passages accentuate God's great holiness, power, and majesty, as well as the reverent fear He instills in all of creation and how nature responds to the awe of His presence. Collectively, they all give us revelation of the Biblical theme of mountains trembling, shaking, and/or quaking in reaction to God's holy and awesome presence.

In getting back to the vision, recall after the tremendous shaking of the mountain, and the ominous feeling as the beautiful skies above became dark and foreboding with flashes of lightning, both bright white and deep red, bouncing around in the blackened clouds that had gathered just over it, I was expecting to see the eruption of a volcano and the spewing of lava. But rather than lava, mud began to spew forth, so much of it, that it caused a massive mountain-wide mudslide. And as the mud rushed down, caught up within it were people of all sorts who were desperately trying to catch themselves from sliding away, but were helpless against the power of the mudslide. I heard the Ancient of Days speak after my trying to understand if this was in reference to the mudslide that recently occurred after the hurricane that hit the Carolinas. He explained to me that He was cleaning the dirt off His Holy Mountain. At this point, I was reminded of the Book of Revelation where Jesus was speaking to the seven different churches of that time. In particular, when He was speaking to the church of Laodicea, also referred to as the lukewarm church in Chapter 3, verses 14-19 NLT.

It reads, "Write this letter to the angel of the church in Laodicea. "This is the message from the one who is the Amen — the faithful and true witness, the beginning of God's new creation: I know all the things you do, that you are neither hot nor cold. I wish that you were one or the other! But since you are like lukewarm water, neither hot nor cold, I will spit (other translations read spew or vomit) you out of my mouth! You say, 'I am rich. I have everything I want. I don't need a thing!' And you don't realize that you are wretched and miserable and poor and blind and naked. So I advise you to buy gold from Me — gold that has been purified by fire. Then you will be rich. Also buy white garments from Me so you will not be shamed by your nakedness, and ointment for your eyes so you will be able to see. I correct and discipline everyone I love. So be diligent and turn from your indifference." Jesus rebuked the people here for their spiritual indifference showing that lukewarmness is unacceptable to God, our Father. He desires either complete commitment or clear rejection of Him and proclaims that spiritual apathy, being wishy-washy, half in and half out is repulsive, sickening, nauseating and is why if not righted, causes the vomiting out. Thus, reminding me of

Jesus vomiting out those who were neither hot nor cold and removing them from His holy mountain, from the muddy mountain. The Scriptures tell us that judgement comes to the house of God first in 1Peter 4:17. It declares, "For the time has come for judgement to begin at the house of God; and if it begins with us first, what will be the end of those who do not obey the gospel of God?"

Now, let's get back to shaking and quaking and take a look at not just the mountains, but the whole earth shaking and quaking at God's visitation and at the miracles that ensued from them as well. The Old Testament has several accounts of earthquakes such as when Korah rebelled against Moses, when Jonathan and his armor bearer attacked the garrison at Gibeah, and during Uzziah's reign, just to mention a few. However, the ones I'd like to draw your attention to are in the New Testament. The first one we'll address is at Jesus' crucifixion and is found in the book of Matthew, chapters 27 and 28.

We find in Matthew 27, verse 46 that as Jesus was hanging on the cross, from the sixth to the ninth hour (from noon until 3 pm in our time) darkness was all over the land. This is the build up and can also be clarified as a miraculous wonder in the earth, but this isn't the half of it. We next find in verses 50-54, that when Jesus died on the cross, and when He was resurrected, there was a great earthquake. Let's look at the verses. "And Jesus cried out with a loud voice, and yielded up His spirit. Then, behold, the veil of the temple was torn in two from top to bottom; and the earth quaked and the rocks were split, and the graves were opened; and many bodies of the saints who had fallen asleep were raised; and coming out of the graves after His resurrection, they went into the holy city and appeared to many. So when the centurion and those with him, who were guarding Jesus, saw the earthquake and the things that had happened, they feared greatly, saying, "Truly this was the Son of God!"

Moving on to Matthew 28, we'll see another earthquake upon Jesus rising from the dead as He's resurrected. It's found in verses 1-4 – "Now after the Sabbath, as the first day of the week began, Mary Magdalene and the other Mary came to see the tomb. And behold, there was a great earthquake; for an angel of the Lord descended from heaven, and came and rolled back the stone from the door, and sat on it. His countenance was like lightning, and his clothing as white as snow." Recounted in the above passages, we see many wondrous miracles following those earthquakes.

In moving further into the New Testament, we find another earthquake in the Book of Acts, chapter 16. After Paul cast a spirit out of a girl who was annoying him, her masters who profited from this and realized their hope of any more profit was now gone, seized Paul and Silas and drug them to the authorities. After Paul and Silas were beaten and imprisoned with their feet fastened into stocks, they began to pray. Let's pick up in verse 25 – But at midnight (the darkest hour of the night) Paul and Silas were praying and singing hymns to God, and the prisoners were listening to them. Suddenly there was a great earthquake, so that the foundations of the prison were shaken; and immediately all the doors were opened and everyone's chains were loosed. Another testimony to the fact that when God visits the earth for whatever reason, shaking earthquakes occur and miracles, signs, and wonders follow! Thank you, Father God.

In Hebrews 12:25-29, we find the Apostle Paul quoting the prophet Haggai and speaking of the latter days of time with both a physical and spiritual shaking. It reads, See that you do not refuse Him who speaks. For if they did not escape who refused Him who spoke on earth, much more shall we not escape if we turn away from Him who speaks from heaven, whose voice then shook the earth; but now He has promised saying, "Yet once more I shake not only the earth, but also heaven." Now this, "Yet once more," indicates the removal of those things that are being shaken, as of the things that are made, that the things which cannot be shaken may remain. Therefore, since we are receiving a kingdom which cannot be shaken, let us have grace, by which we may serve God acceptably with reverence and godly fear. For our God is a consuming fire. – Here Paul is encouraging us to hear and heed God's heavenly voice for there is a shaking coming that no one will be able to avoid.

Right now, in our present time, we are experiencing a shaking from God as indicated by both the snowy mountain and the muddy mountain visions. Let's take a closer look at some of this shaking. One thing in particular that was a worldwide global shaking, was Covid 19. It hit and affected every single nation on earth. And since this pestilence hit, so many things have been shaken out, so many things brought to light that were hiding in darkness. This should not be a surprise because Jesus did proclaim in Luke 12:2-3 NLT – "The time is coming when everything that is covered up will be revealed, and all that is secret will be made known to all." Covid most certainly was a catalyst for the beginning stages of this! Still to this very day, previously hidden deeds are still coming to light and are being shouted from the rooftops through various types of media coverage. We have seen prominent figures in the church and Christian music fall, to mention just a few instances, because of hidden sin being brought to light as God cleans His holy mountain. This shaking and revealing is happening in many other areas of the secular world too, like that of a music mogul, a prominent businessman, also, some public figures in the sports arena have fallen in disgrace. Similarly, a wide variety of men and women in many stations of our government are being exposed for backhandedness. So many illegal and backhanded deals were done under the cover of the shutdown of Covid 19, even including data about its very origins. So much of this evil is still being discovered and revealed to this present day, six years later. One such example is the fraud in Minnesota involving day care centers that cost taxpayers an estimated 9 billion dollars at last check.

This shaking most assuredly has made many aware that they no longer can look at the government as a source of confidence as far as it being good for the people. People voted in officials they trusted to make good moral decisions for the people, but morality had no importance in the decisions they made. Also, there is no longer a confidence in government in the arena of economics either. Government officials all over the world, as well as in our country, cannot fix the inflation that is spiraling out of control. Even decisions with the very best of intents from those whom we considered very wise and knowledgeable in economics, just cannot get a handle on the climbing inflationary conditions we're currently living in.

Let's now explore some of the good that came from this pestilence known as Covid 19, before we continue more about this shaking. While our government put us all in lockdown, parents discovered the unholy filth that was being taught in their children's classrooms as the children not having the one-on-one help from their teachers or even their fellow classmates was passed on to them. Parents learned that in the schools, immorality and "woke ideologies" were being taught. Kids were being taught there really wasn't only two sexes, that they didn't have to be the gender they were born as, encouraging homosexuality, transgenderism, and putting mental pressure on them to choose pronouns. Filling their minds with insane things such as they could be whatever they wanted to identify as, even if it was a cat. The kids were taught that their own feelings were to be their guiding light regardless of what anyone else says or thinks, encouraging selfishness as well as disbelieving Biblical truths. Oh, and children as young as kindergarteners were being taught some of these things by drag queens! Complete depravity!

However, what happened since then, is that parents started pulling their children from the public schools and either enrolling them in private Christian schools or began homeschooling their children, teaching the Word of God along with the fundamentals, and even out of that, homeschooling co-ops have been formed. Enrollments in both of the above have been increasing exponentially since then. Praise God! Also, during the frightening isolation, many began to call out to God, seeking Him for so many things and therefore, personal relationships with God were strengthened, and some, after crying out for answers and help, met God for the first time right there in their own homes, and began their journey with Jesus as their Lord and Savior. Then when things were opened again, the churches saw more and more people attending churches worldwide. See, the fear of death, which Covid 19 brought, is always a catalyst of spiritual awakening.

On top of all of this, people began to realize that those they thought were important in their lives, really were not, whether they were secular musicians, movie and television stars, models, etc. as the music, movie, and television industries came to a screeching halt in Hollywood and beyond. Many learned to be better stewards of their money discovering that it really wasn't that bad to go without some things they previously couldn't live without, having the latest, newest, and greatest version of (fill in the blank). Toilet paper was much more valuable than those things. And most importantly, people learned that there was a big world out there, full of people just as vulnerable as they were, and got them to consider others, instead of living in their own little self-centered world.

In getting back to shaking, we find Paul speaking of a Spiritual shaking while writing to Timothy in 2 Timothy 3:1 NLT – "You should know this Timothy, that in the last days there will be very difficult times. For people will love only themselves and their money. They will be boastful and proud, scoffing at God, disobedient to their parents, and ungrateful. They will consider nothing sacred. They will be unloving and unforgiving; they will slander others and have no self-control. They will be cruel and hate what is good. They will betray their friends, be reckless, be puffed up with pride, and love pleasure rather than God." It's very safe to say we are living in very difficult times right now and therefore are experiencing a Spiritual shaking of the earth.

We'll now examine some other things Jesus said concerning the latter days, to help us see the days we are living in. He foretells in Luke 21:8-11, the upcoming upheaval the earth will experience. – And He said: "Take heed that you not be deceived…But when you hear of wars and commotions, do not be terrified; for these things must come to pass first, but the end will not come immediately." Then He said to them, "Nation will rise against nation, and kingdom against kingdom. And there will be great earthquakes in various places, and famines and pestilences; and there will be fearful sights and great signs from heaven."

We've heard of wars and rumors of wars for further back than the span of my lifetime so this is nothing new. However, I want to discuss a couple of recent ones. The war between Hamas and Israel first, only to take note that several peace treaties/ceasefires were set up and broken in that war before this last one, and God only knows if it will be sustained, or yet again, is temporary, for He knows all things. And unfortunately, we all watched as famine swept through the Gaza Strip because of this war. The second war I'd like to discuss is between Russia and Ukraine where a peace treaty/ceasefire has not been able to be forged. And because of other world power countries looking at this, they have their eyes on countries they want to attack for more land too, and are just being watchful to see what the rest of the powerful countries would potentially do about it. These are our commotions between countries and rumors of wars, not to mention many countries having nuclear weapons. That alone, within itself, is more than a commotion or rumor of war, but a threat of war for total annihilation of any foes.

We've already discussed earthquakes but let's couple "earthquakes in various places" hinting at places where they are not normally seen, with "there will be fearful sights and great signs from heaven." I want to present to you the expansion of earthquakes in various places to also include other naturally occurring weather events, particularly unprecedented weather phenomenon in the heavens. We are experiencing great floods where floods don't commonly occur, hurricanes where hurricanes outside of presently known hurricane paths have arrived and wreaked havoc, like the previously mentioned hurricane-instigated mudslide in North Carolina. As well as these hurricanes being historically more potent. Also, a volcano in Ethiopia named Hayli Gubbi, erupted for the first time in recorded history on November 23rd, 2025!

Conspiracy theorists claim that HAARP (high-frequency active auroral research program) is responsible for the weather phenomenon of floods, etc. occurring in unusual places because it's a powerful weather manipulation tool and works alongside cloud seeding. I'm not going to say whether it is or isn't, simply because I honestly don't know. But what I do want to say is, I hope and pray that we would not be so foolish as to not understand that God is all knowing and is the one who tells us things before they happen, knowing the beginning from the end. So, if HAARP is as suggested, God would have known man would develop this technology, as it is said in Timothy, that man would ever be increasing in knowledge and never learning the truth. Therefore, let us not scoff at such weather and nature related things as not being from God and prophecy being fulfilled. God rules the heavens and all that happen there including the weather!

Let's now look at Luke 21:11 from a symbolic, spiritual perspective with "there will be great earthquakes in various places, and famines and pestilences; and there will be fearful sights and great signs from heaven" also referencing spiritual, symbolic upheavals and disruptions. Let's view earthquakes with not only literal shaking, but a shaking of societal and spiritual unrest, shaking the very foundations of our human existence here on earth. The increase of antisemitism and Christian persecutions, as a couple of facets of this. Also, at famines and pestilences as indicative of just not physical hunger and disease only, but as spiritual depravity, and of suffering being symptomatic of all the various challenges we are yet to face. Let it be a challenge for us to be fully prepared for any and every thing that may come our way while we await the return of our Bridegroom as discussed in a parable in the last chapter. And lastly, let's look at Jesus' warning about fearful sights and great signs from heaven as being extraordinary happenings evoking both wonder and fear, as merely pointing to divine intervention and the fulfillment of prophecies, urging us to stand firm in our faith amidst chaos and God's shaking the world. Not to catapult the saints of God into fear, but to remind us of Jesus, our blessed assurance, when we belong to Him. May we allow all of this to encourage us to face worldly uncertainty with hope, preparedness, and perseverance together, in the unity of Christ, just as we did during the shaking of Covid 19. Amen!

In conclusion of this chapter, I'd like to share another vision the Lord gave me to help cement the meaning of the vision of the muddy mountain in the beginning of this chapter. I was shown a vision of the earth as a globe and as I was looking at it, a white linen sheet or table cloth appeared over the earth. It was firm and straight as though sitting on a flat surface such as a table, but it wasn't, there was nothing immediately beneath it, just the earth further below and certainly not flat. Upon the sheet/table cloth, were small wooden carved figurines of men and women wearing various clothing, representing different careers or stations in life. Some were clothed in business attire, some in jogging suits, and some were in jeans and flannel shirts. The women were in business skirts and jackets while others were in slacks and sweaters, and others still, in jeans and t-shirts or sweatshirts. Some were carrying briefcases, some purses, and some, nothing at all. I then heard the Spirit tell me to take a closer look and observe the coloring of all these pieces. I then noticed that all the wood carvings were in varied shades of colors like cream, beige, tan, brown, and dark brown, as though representing wood that came from many different regions of the earth, as well as the people being from many varied countries. All of them reminded me of homemade carved or whittled chess pieces.

Suddenly, the flat sheet was lifted up with invisible hands and then shook like when one is putting new bedclothes on a bed, creating ripples. During this, some of the wooden figures flew right off. While trying to understand this, that process of shaking out was repeated with more of the figures flying off. This scene was repeated several more times, until there were significantly fewer figurines left. The last few times the white cloth was shaken, some figures fell against others, broke into two pieces, and then flew off. When I studied the fewer remaining figurines, I then heard the Lord speak again, saying, "May I introduce to you, My remnant!"

I was later reminded of the Scripture passages that refer to Jesus as the rejected stone of the builders, but now is the chief cornerstone, that He will become a stumbling stone to some and that whoever falls on this stone will be broken. These references, among others, can be found in both The Old and The New Testaments in Isaiah 8:14-15, Psalm118:22-23, Romans 9:32-33 and 1 Peter 2:7-8 which clarifies that they stumble because of their unbelief. May we all hear what the Spirit is teaching, see what He is showing us, and pray He reveals to each of us, individually, what He would have us to do, just like He did to the seven churches of Revelation. Amen!

Zephaniah 3:11-13 NLT – "…I will remove all proud and arrogant people from among you. There will be no more haughtiness on My holy mountain. Those who are left will be lowly and humble, for they trust in the name of the LORD. The remnant …will do no wrong; they will never tell lies or deceive one another. They will eat and sleep in safety, and no one will make them afraid."

CHAPTER SIX

THE FLOURISHING TIME-LAPSE MOUNTAIN

Recall at the beginning of this vision, the entirety of the mudslide and people that had been caught up in it disappeared from the bottom of the mountain. Then once more and again, the mountain was devoid of everything and just composed of toffee-brown colored dirt. As I contemplated this, I heard in the Spirit, the words – "It is a new day!" And as I heard those words, I was reminded of the mountain beginning to grow greenery, all types of foliage, vegetation, plants, and trees as if watching a time-lapse video. They were sprouting up all over the whole mountain. It reminded me of in the Book of Genesis when God was creating the heavens and earth in that new day, the third day. In Genesis 1:11-13 NLT, it declares – Then God said, "Let the land sprout forth with vegetation—every sort of seed-bearing plant, and trees that grow seed-bearing fruit. These seeds will then produce the kinds of plants and trees from which they came." And that is what happened. The land produced vegetation— all sorts of seed-bearing plants, and trees with seed-bearing fruit. Their seeds produced plants and trees of the same kind. And God saw that it was good. And evening passed and morning came, marking the third day. And that is precisely what happened here in this vision.

The third day holds great pertinence throughout the Holy Bible, so we would be remiss if we didn't explore and touch on some of these references as the Holy Spirit has revealed its importance in this installment of the vision. I touched on the third day in my book "Journey To The Mountaintop" emphasizing gaining a new spiritual perspective, being able to spiritually see things we've not seen before with the example of after three days, the scales fell from Saul's eyes after he was blinded during his Damascus Road encounter with Jesus. It can be found in Acts 9. We also glean other aspects of the third day throughout the Scriptures and we'll touch on a few of them so we can understand what the Ancient of Days is revealing to us. The third day signifies new beginnings, renewal, transformation, resurrection, bringing new life, and divine protection. In Hosea 6:1-3 NKJV, we find – Come and let us return to the LORD; For He has torn, but He will heal us; He has stricken, but He will bind us up. After two days He will revive us; On the third day He will raise us up, That we may live in His sight. Let us know, Let us pursue the knowledge of the LORD. His going forth is established in the morning; He will come to us like the rain, like the latter and former rain to the earth.

We also find another important aspect of the third day in Exodus 19:10-11 NKJV. Here we find God promises to visit the earth on top of Mount Sinai in the sight of all the people, and everyone will see and know He is visiting and had better prepare themselves for the third day by being consecrated or sanctified and washing their garments clean. It reads, - Then the Lord said to Moses, "Go to the people and consecrate them today and tomorrow, and let them wash their clothes. And let them be ready for the third day. For on the third day the Lord will come down on Mount Sinai in the sight of all the people." The washing of their garments characterizes an outward act of cleansing that was to represent their inward desire to be holy and set apart for God's sacred purposes. And what I find interesting, is that God would visit and all the people would see Him. Let us have ears to hear and eyes to see what the Spirit is speaking and doing!

Next, let's look at Joshua 1:10-11 NLT – Joshua then commanded the officers of Isreal, "Go through the camp and tell the people to get their provisions ready. In three days you will cross the Jordan River and take possession of the land the LORD your God is giving you." What I wanted you to note from this example is yet another instruction to be ready and make sure you have provisions for when the Lord moves, like at Mount Sinai above, and the parable of the ten bridesmaids from Chapter 4. And lastly, of course, we have many Biblical references to Jesus rising from the dead on the third day speaking of resurrection power. Before moving on, there's one more thing that I find noteworthy. It's that throughout these examples we see new life emerging from times of chaos on or in the third day.

I also received the Scripture passage Isaiah 43:19-20 NLT – For I am about to do something new. See, I have already begun! Do you not see it? I will make a pathway through the wilderness. I will create rivers in the dry wasteland. The wild animals in the fields will thank Me, the jackals and owls, too, for giving them water in the desert. Yes, I will make rivers in the dry wasteland so my chosen people can be refreshed.

Other Scripture that pertain to the imagery in this vision are Ezekiel 47:12 NLT – "Fruit trees of all kinds will grow along both sides of the river. The leaves of these trees will never turn brown and fall, and there will always be fruit on their branches. There will be a new crop every month, for they are watered by the river flowing from the Temple. The fruit will be good for food and the leaves for healing." Jeremiah 17:7-8 NLT – "But blessed are those who trust in the Lord and have made the Lord their hope and confidence. They are like trees planted along a riverbank, with roots that reach deep into the water. Such trees are not bothered by the heat or worried by long months of drought. Their leaves stay green, and they never stop producing fruit." Another potent one is found in Psalm 1:1, 3 NLT – Oh, the joys of those who do not follow the advice of the wicked, or stand around with sinners, or join in with mockers…They are like trees planted along the riverbank, bearing fruit each season. Their leaves never wither, and they prosper in all they do. And of course, Revelation 22:2 NLT – Then the angel showed me a river with the water of life, clear as crystal, flowing from the throne of God and of the Lamb. It flowed down the center of the main street. On each side of the river grew a tree of life, bearing twelve crops of fruit, with a fresh crop each month. The leaves were used for medicine to heal the nations.

Let's now examine the Scripture verses in the above-mentioned Ezekiel and Jeremiah verses. When these prophecies were given at that time in ancient culture, they had a great implication that we may not completely comprehend today. Back then, there were no pharmaceutical companies that produced a slew of medications for all types of ailments, no pharmacies, no doctor's offices, no urgent cares centers found at just about every corner, and no emergency rooms. They had no telehealth portals at their fingertips to use to get instructions and prescriptions for relief from disorders, sicknesses, or diseases. There were no scientific labs to test and create medications. Technology is increasing so exponentially as time marches on, it's incredible! The newest medical technology to be released is ChatGPT Health. But, what the people of this Biblical time had to rely on were leaves, herbs, and fruits for healing, valued for their medicinal properties, provided for them by God. The Bible does give us many examples of these in the Scriptures, which we'll cover in just a bit to bring out several points. But before we do that, I want to share with you an incident from my childhood that shows it wasn't too far in the distant past that these natural methods were still being relied upon and used.

It was the mid-1960s and I was just a little girl. My grandmother, my mom's mom, was from what she referred to as the 'old country': Levoča, Czechoslovakia to be exact. She moved to the United States when she was a young teenager back in the mid-1930s. So only approximately 30 years had passed since her arrival when this incident took place. Mom and Grandma had planned a day where we would come and visit her while my dad was at work. Unfortunately, my sister had developed an earache overnight. This didn't stop us from visiting Grandma though, because Mom knew Grandma could help alleviate my sister's pain from past experience while growing up and my sister did not have a fever, so the visit was still on. So, once we arrived and Mom shared with Grandma that my sister had an earache, Grandma went into action. She promptly went out through the side door just off the kitchen and into her little herb garden. She returned with a cluster of little leaves in the palm of her cupped hand.

It was at this point that all chaos broke out. My grandma wanted to put those leaves inside my sister's ear and my sister freaked out, jumped off the couch, and started running. Grandma started running too, trying to chase her down. My sister was frantically and fearfully running in circles around the coffee table in front of the couch and Grandma was close behind. I didn't know whether to laugh because it looked so funny, or to be frightened because my sister was so afraid. So, I did the only thing I could think of to do. I just pulled my legs up in front of me while sitting on the couch so they wouldn't be bumped into by either my sister or my grandmother and just watched as they went around and around the coffee table. Funny how memories are. I don't recall what those leaves were or if Grandma ever got those leaves inside my sister's ear and if she was able to, if it even helped. The only thing I do remember after that is the whole incident spawning a nightmare. My sister had a bad dream that Grandma was a witch doctor and she was afraid of Grandma for a while after that. I guess that's what happens when a child is used to getting medicine from a doctor when she is sick, and perhaps a vivid imagination, or even too much television. Anyway, my whole point in sharing that memory was to illustrate that it wasn't too long ago when people relied on what God has provided us in nature to take care of many of our healing needs. There is even a push in getting back to that, in some circles, with what is called holistic healing.

Getting back to Scripture references of the medicinal properties of plants, leaves, and fruit, we find in 2 Kings 20:1, 4-7 – About that time Hezekiah became deathly ill, and the prophet Isaiah son of Amoz went to visit him…This is what the LORD, the God of your ancestor David says: I have heard your prayer and seen your tears. I will heal you, and three days from now you will get out of bed and go to the Temple of the LORD. I will add fifteen years to your life…Then Isaiah said, "Make an ointment from figs." So Hezekiah's servants spread the ointment over the boil, and Hezekiah recovered! Figs have medicinal properties and when applied to an infected area in an ointment or poultice, are able to draw toxins out. In Mark 4:30-31, the mustard seed is mentioned. It was known to also have medicinal properties in that mustard was used as a stimulant and for treating respiratory issues. Its warming properties were believed to assist in circulation and alleviate chest congestion.

Another reference is that of the pomegranate mentioned in many Scripture passages. It was valued for the medicinal properties of its seeds known for their antioxidant properties and for its juice and extracts as having anti-inflammatory and antimicrobial properties. Also, hyssop is mentioned in Psalm 51:7 and was revered for its medicinal properties of being an antiseptic and expectorant which assisted in cleansing wounds and treating respiratory conditions. We can't move on without mentioning the medicinal properties of grapes/wine. We know the good Samaritan treated a man with wine to cleanse his wounds and that Paul instructed Timothy to drink a little small dose of wine to help him with his digestive issues.

The above references are but a few, however, what I want to draw your attention to is that as with every plant, there is a season for planting and a season for harvesting. During the harvesting season, all the plants, leaves and fruits would be in abundance, however, as time moved on, they would be more difficult to come by for as time passed, they were out of season. Much of them had already been consumed and finding the preserved ones became more difficult, for they were scarce and expensive if one wanted to purchase them. So, when the people in the time of the prophets first heard the words of Ezekiel – "Fruit trees of all kinds will grow along both sides of the river. The leaves of these trees will never turn brown and fall, and there will always be fruit on their branches. There will be a new crop every month, for they are watered by the river flowing from the Temple. The fruit will be good for food and the leaves for healing." And those from Jeremiah – "But blessed are those who trust in the Lord and have made the Lord their hope and confidence. They are like trees planted along a riverbank, with roots that reach deep into the water. Such trees are not bothered by the heat or worried by long months of drought. Their leaves stay green, and they never stop producing fruit." The people understood that there would never be an "out of season." There would always be these medicinal plants, trees, and leaves available, they would always be convenient, always be in abundance in good times and in bad. How wonderful to know that healing would always be available. In the original language spoken, the words "in season and out of season" found in 2 Timothy 4:2 mean "timely and untimely", or "convenient and inconvenient". The word for "in season" literally means "good time." And "out of season" comes from the same word but with a different prefix, giving it the opposite meaning, "not a good time." So, there is never a "not a good time" for receiving healing just as there is never a "not a good time' for sharing the gospel.

All of this is what was represented in this installment of the vision where the people beneath the trees looked weary and disheveled and then were transformed as they began to partake of the various types of fruit. It then looked like their clothing had been laundered and pressed. They now appeared fresh and energized. And the one woman in particular biting into a leaf she had plucked from a branch of the tree and getting a look of pure joy on her face, touching her forehead, cheeks, and neck, lifting up her arms and surveying them, noting she was healed. And this also makes the Spiritual meaning of this all the more potent for us as well, as we recognize what the Spirit is showing us regarding the times we are living in. We not only have the promise of physical healing, but healing of our emotional wounds, our mental wounds, and our spiritual wounds. No more suffering for long periods of time with crushed, or heavy spirits! In essence we have total healing, body, soul, and spirit available to us at all times, morning, noon, and night! Thank you, Jesus!

Next, let's delve into a deeper focus on what trees planted by the water means and what the Spirit is urging us to do with this vision installment. Trees planted by the water stand strong, drawing nourishment via their roots drinking in from Jesus, the life-giving water the trees are planted next to. In the same way, we as believers are instructed to seek strength and nourishment through drinking in God's Word and His presence. Being planted by His water ensures us wholeness and the ability to stay rooted and grounded in Him even in times of turmoil and chaos. Trees planted by the water are known to bear fruit in every season and God asks us to bear good fruit in every kind of season whether they are times of blessing or times of trying. He equips us through His Word to be emotionally stable regardless of what's going on around us.

Being trees planted alongside the river of life also assures us that we can stand tall and strong in Him no matter the seasons of life, through high winds, pelting rains, or unexpected drought. It also ensures us of joy. As we immerse ourselves in His presence, His

Word, and via prayer, we experience a deep-rooted joy. A joy that sustains us and nourishes our spirits as water and roots nourish trees. We are assured that during difficult times we are never alone which feeds our lives with faith, hope, happiness, and satisfaction. Also, the picture of trees planted by the waters represents God-given grace throughout our journey with Him. His grace assures us that we are never alone and equips us with the ability to stay grounded in Him no matter what life may throw our way.

If you'll notice, all of the above benefits are benefits that we receive from God; we, ourselves, us, or in the singular, I. But God doesn't want it to end there. Yes, these are all benefits the Lord gives to us and are most assuredly a very important part of our walk with Him. But in getting back to the vision, we'll pick up at the part where the woman partook of the leaf and received healing and refresh our memories as to what happened next. In the vision I saw, she suddenly began to pull more leaves from the tree and drop them into an apron pocket. As she did so, I was able to somehow see into her mind, and I saw images of different people's faces flash across her forehead. I then just instantaneously knew she was thinking of others who she wanted to share these leaves with. And that is what the Spirit of God is calling for during His great and mighty visitation upon the earth right now. We, whom God has called to be mature sons in the earth, are to go forth and share what we have received from Him. I hear in the Spirit that the time is ripe, our fruit is matured and ripe. It's time to go forth and let our light shine before men so that the glory of the Lord may be seen upon us and that they may see our good works, our good fruit, and glorify our Father in heaven!

I heard the Spirit say to His church, the Body of Christ, His remnant, "Even as I have poured into you, it is time for you to pour into others." As I heard the Spirit speak, I had a vision of the heavens open up and saw hands holding a vessel. The vessel was dazzling, made from pure gold, and had a midnight blue background and a brilliant design reminding me of looking at a galaxy of stars, and other glittery stars and planets that covered the vessel all the way around. These were all sparkling gold and silver including the swirls around them. Suddenly, they were no longer stationary, but began to move as though they were alive.

Next, the hands tipped the vessel slightly and pure glistening water began to pour forth from it. As I watched the water spill, I saw it fill up other vessels, and when these vessels were full, they began to tip and spill as well. From atop a very fertile mountain, they became cascading waterfalls of many different widths and depths. As I watched these waterfalls go forth all over the earth, the view changed from up close to further back. It's rather difficult to explain, but it was as if I was viewing up close and the whole earth all at once. Anyway, as I watched these cascading waterfalls continuing on, I realized they were flowing around the entire earth and when they came back around to where they began, I saw an extremely wide river with trees planted along both sides with branches so heavy laden with fruit, that the branches touched the ground, making the side-by-side trees then resemble arches you could walk through and go right up to the river. It all appeared as an inviting garden that had everything anyone could ever want or need and was truly a breathtaking sight to see.

At that point, I once again saw a part of the flourishing mountain vision. It was the part where I observed many streams and rivers cascading down the mountainside in between many jungles, forests, meadows, and fields. I now recognized those as tributaries, branches, and offshoots from the one large river also feeding the earth and causing the land to sprout forth with vegetation—every sort of seed-bearing plant, and trees that grow seed-bearing fruit. These seeds were then producing the kinds of plants and trees from which they came. These represent the chosen ones of God pouring out to others as the Spirit instructed us to do, and so on, and so on. I was reminded of Matthew 24:14 NLT where Jesus explained to His disciples – "And the Good News about the Kingdom will be preached throughout the whole world, so that all nations will hear it; and then the end will come." And of the afore-mentioned Revelation 22:2 NLT passage – Then the angel showed me a river with the water of life, clear as crystal, flowing from the throne of God and of the Lamb. It flowed down the center of the main street. On each side of the river grew a tree of life, bearing twelve crops of fruit, with a fresh crop each month. The leaves were used for medicine to heal the nations.

Saints of God, we are living in an unprecedented time with this great visitation upon the earth. The heavens are open over us to ask and receive, for doors of opportunity to be opened for furthering and expanding the Kingdom of God. God is opening doors that no man can shut and shutting doors that no man can open. May we go forth in our God-given calling and heed the great commission of Jesus. Matthew 28:18-19 NLT – "I have been given all authority in heaven and on earth. Therefore, go and make disciples of all nations, baptizing them in the name of the Father and of the Son and the Holy Spirit." And I say, Amen!

CHAPTER SEVEN

THE OIL LAMPS UPON THE MOUNTAIN

If you'll recall, in the beginning of the installment of this vision, I was taken to a place on the mountain at street level. As I began to take in the scenery, I noted that all of the houses that lined the street appeared to be from the 1800s, then, as if to confirm the time period, I witnessed a woman pass me by as she was walking down the street. She was clothed in a light blue long hoop dress, full from her small waist down, with lace adorning the close-fitting top of the dress. Her hair was pinned up high on her head with one elegant banana curl adorning one side. She was holding up a matching parasol over herself to protect her fair complexion from the sun. I knew that if the Holy Spirit was showing me the era and a woman from it, that it must hold some significance of what He wanted me to understand in regards to this segment of the ongoing vision.

I recalled in a class on church history I took at my church, that the 1800s were in what is called the Second Great Awakening in the United States. So, I prayerfully did some research on it. One of the things that really struck me was this Second Great Awakening especially appealed to women and the focus on women was prominent. In fact, the majority of converts during this Great Awakening were women. Religious meetings provided women who were heretofore often sidelined in traditional religious settings, with fantastic opportunities for public speaking and utilizing their organizational skills. Some of the greatest strides for women entering into the public arena came from their work in forming and sustaining societies directed at social reform and aimed at bettering life in the United States not only for women, but for slaves, and children as well. One of the great things that came from the women's work, was the fight for women's rights later becoming known as suffrage, and led to women's right to vote.

Women also were significant in organizing and teaching Sunday School classes after the forming of The Sunday School Union.

Through all of this, women also became missionaries and preachers, called to evangelize the nation before Jesus' second coming and is still ongoing today. I'm sure we can all think of a woman, or many women even, who have been called, chosen, and anointed by God who obeyed His call and did amazing things for the Kingdom of God. And that's not even mentioning all of the women God used throughout the Bible. However, this movement during the Second Great Awakening, didn't come without great resistance from some men who adamantly believed that women should not preach the Gospel. But the prevailing argument to that, if you will, was – Why should it be forbidden for women to preach, seeing as how our Lord and Savior Jesus Christ died for both men and women alike? And I say, Well…

Society has come a long way since then in regards to women doing the Lord's work and preaching or teaching messages in public and in churches. But there is always room for improvement in the Kingdom until Jesus has brought it to completion. As a matter of fact, it was approximately 30 years ago when at my old church, there was this woman, who shall remain nameless, who spoke at a conference our church put on. Afterward, a pastor of a neighboring church approached her and asked her if she would be interested in sharing what she had spoken on, in his church at a Sunday night service. Now mind you, this pastor believed that women should not preach the Gospel, so when it came time to have her speak, he said to his congregation, "Tonight, we're going to have Sister "Nameless" come up and just say something." And she preached the message God had given her. I found this to be quite humorous. This is also why God is calling for mindset changes in this time and leading us to examine whether what we are walking in is actually according to His Word, or is merely a tradition of men we've picked up along the way.

When God anoints someone, He, in a sense, has made them to be a light in the world, in the thing He anointed them for. Like Jesus said in Matthew 5:14-15 NKJV – "You are the light of the world. A city that is set on a hill cannot be hidden. Nor do they light a lamp and put it under a basket, but on a lampstand, and it gives light to all

who are in the house. And this brings us to the lampstand or oil lamp in the vision. What happened next was I noticed a street lamp and
while I was checking it out, noticed that it appeared old fashioned;
nothing like the street lights we see today. Dusk fell and it
illuminated. That's when I realized this street lamp wasn't electric with an incandescent bulb, but was in fact, an oil lamp. I wasn't clear on what the Lord wanted me to understand about this, but knew it held great significance.

Then, once more and again, I was given another segment of the vision with the oil lamp, but with other important elements as well. Recollect that in the last installment of this ongoing vision, I saw the same street and oil lamp but the scenery had changed to a different era. I once again saw a lady walking down the street. But this time the lady was walking a cute little dog on a red leash down the road. However, her clothing identified the time period to be that of the 1960s. I found this extremely interesting because the 1960s was a time when the women of society were crying out for equal rights in the business place, equal pay for equal work, etc. I believe it was an outward expression of even what the spirits of women were craving, as the Holy Spirit was stirring up the gifting within them, if you will. And it was in 1960 when the Charismatic Movement began which furthered the movement of women having leadership roles in the church as well as being permitted to use their gifting within the church. The two prominent Scriptures being Joel 2:28 – And it shall come to pass afterward that I will pour out My Spirit on all flesh; your sons and your daughters shall prophesy…And Galatians 3:28 – There is neither Jew nor Greek, there is neither slave nor free, there is neither male nor female; for you are all one in Christ Jesus. It also referenced Debroah the judge from the Old Testament and Phoebe in a leadership role from the New Testament. In seeing that the Holy Spirit brought emphasis on women in both of these, I am confident He is revealing to us that He is continuing His plan and anointed women will play a substantial role in this current visitation upon the earth. One more thing I'd like to highlight about the 60s before moving on is that it also was a time of civil unrest with riots and violence in the streets like we are seeing today. An indication of shaking and pressure upon the earth.

In getting back to the oil lamp, as I was studying it, dusk fell again and it lit up once more, then suddenly intensified in the light it was throwing. I thought that darkness had fallen now and that was the reason for the brighter light, but upon looking skyward, realized it hadn't darkened at all, but that the lamp had more oil. As I was pondering over what the Holy Spirit wanted me to know from this, I heard Him speak. He explicitly said, "In this season, the tool in My hand is the oil press. Just as I used Satan as a tool to bring My servant Job to a closer relationship with Me and to bring him more knowledge of who I am in the Old Testament, and just as I used Satan as a tool to mature Peter and teach Him that He cannot do what I called him to do in His own power and might in the New Testament, so am I continuing and using Satan now in this day by allowing him to work his evil, spread his lies, and work those who listen to him up in a frenzy for the purpose of putting pressure upon the earth. I have set parameters of what he can and cannot do just as I did with Job. But this pressing is what brings forth the olive oil. I am producing more oil in this way as this is a time where I am bringing many of my sons to maturity and am highlighting the anointing of My anointed ones, that they may draw men unto Me. This pressure is causing the fields of the earth to be ripe for harvest. Don't be anxious or dismayed, for what the enemy means for evil, I turn around for good. I work all things together for good for those who love Me and are called, chosen, and anointed according to My purposes." Thank you, Father!

After the Holy Spirit spoke this to me, I kept hearing, "Jesus in the garden. Jesus in the garden." So, I turned in my Bible to when Jesus was praying in the Garden of Gethsemane, also referred to as the Mount of Olives, and this is key, for in the original Greek, Gethsemane literally means oil press. It is purposely mentioned in the context of Jesus' prayer and preparation for His impending sacrifice just before His crucifixion. Let's look at the account found in Matthew 26:36-46 NLT – Then Jesus went with them to the olive grove called Gethsemane, and He said, "Sit here while I go over there to pray." He took Peter and Zebedee's two sons, James and John, and He became anguished and distressed. He told them "My soul is crushed with grief to the point of death. Stay here and keep watch with Me." He went on a little further and bowed with his face to the ground, praying, "My Father! If it is possible, let this cup of suffering be taken away from Me. Yet I want Your will to be done, not Mine." Then He returned to the disciples and found them asleep. He said to Peter, "Couldn't you watch with Me even one hour?' Keep watch and pray so that you will not give in to temptation. For the spirit is willing, but the body is weak!" Then Jesus left them a second time and prayed. "My Father! If this cup cannot be taken away unless I drink it, Your will be done." When He returned to them again, He found them sleeping, for they couldn't keep their eyes open. So He went to pray a third time, saying the same things again. Then He came to the disciples and said, "Go ahead and sleep. Have your rest. But look—the time has come. The Son of Man is betrayed into the hands of sinners. Up, let's be going. Look, my betrayer is here!"

What we learn here is that the oil press reveals the spiritual principle of transformation through pressure as so concisely shown through Jesus' struggle and prayer. See, just as olives must be crushed to produce oil, we believers must suffer life's pressures and then surrender to God's will in order to release the anointing that God has given us. Also, life's pressures and turmoil likewise serve the people of the world who have been called and chosen but have not yet accepted the salvation they're called to by bringing them to the end of themselves as the pressure mounts and they can barely handle it anymore. It is at that point many do cry out to the God they've heard of, but have not yet believed in, until possibly now. And when He personally answers their cry of help by whatever means He deems best for them, whether it be a saint sent to them or He Himself speaking to them, they believe, and then they receive Jesus as their Lord and Savior and at that point are also transformed. Let us remember and be encouraged by the knowledge that God is allowing this pressure upon His saints to release what He has placed within us, and for the people of the world to accept the invitation that God has extended to them.

Let us understand that the crushing of the olives represents the trials and challenges we are facing in life. And the pressing signifies the refining of our characters and the purifying of our souls. Also, the extraction of the oil indicates our inner transformation and spiritual growth and maturity and the releasing of the oil as the anointing of the Holy Spirit, as well as the presence of God manifest in our lives. And lastly, that the light produced by the oil symbolizes God, through His Holy Spirit, illuminating His Word to and through us as we are guided by Him in the very thing He created us for.

What we need to remember as we are going through the oil press process is 2 Corinthians 4:8-9 NKJV – We are hard-pressed on every side, yet not crushed; we are perplexed, but not in despair; persecuted, but not forsaken; struck down but not destroyed… Let this verse encourage us in that when we are being pressed, it isn't proof of failure on our part, but proof of being chosen by God and if we trust Him in it, His grace will bring us through it empowered by His Holy Spirit. As we perhaps feel a hidden private weight of the calling upon us leading to loneliness or loss at times, or times of wrestling with our call, or even ridicule from some who are near and dear to us, know this doesn't mean that we are weak, it means that we are sealed as God's own. Know that going through the press is where the anointing is produced and perfected and via that anointing, we could break chains of addiction, heal broken hearts, or even feed the nations according to what our call is as the Holy Spirit works through us.

More oil represents more anointing being released in this time and season of God's visitation. We were anointed for all of what God created us to be and do before we were born, but God had planned times and seasons for that anointing to be released. As Ecclesiastes 3:1 teaches – To everything there is a season, A time for every purpose under heaven. We can look at the life of Jesus to learn what the Holy Spirit is teaching here. Jesus was born the "anointed one" but He knew there was a time for Him to move in particular anointings. The Book of John records that Jesus, His mother, and His disciples were invited to a wedding at Cana on the third day. Let's not let the importance of the third day escape us here. During the festivities, the wine supply ran out and out of concern for the reputation of those putting on the wedding celebration, Jesus' mom told Jesus that they had no more wine. He replied telling His mother that this was not their problem. He then stated that His time had not come. If you continue reading the account, you'll find that Jesus turned water into wine. In that moment, the anointing to perform this miracle was released. However, His greater anointing that covered even more wasn't released until later. First, He was led into the desert to be tempted by Satan after fasting for forty days and forty nights. A pressure on Him for sure. No doubt His mortal body was in a weakened state. After He prevailed over the temptations presented Him, Jesus then returned to Galilee filled with the Holy Spirit's power. He returned to His boyhood home of Nazareth and it is here we find the greater anointing release in the synagogue there.

Luke 4:17-21 NKJV – And He was handed the book of the prophet Isaiah. And when He had opened the book, He found the place where it was written: "The Spirit of the Lord is upon Me, Because He has anointed Me To preach the gospel to the poor; He has sent Me to heal the brokenhearted, To proclaim liberty to the captives And recovery of sight to the blind, To set at liberty those who are oppressed; To proclaim the acceptable year of the Lord." Then He closed the book, gave it back to the attendant and sat down. And the eyes of all who were in the synagogue were fixed on Him. And He began to say to them, "Today this Scripture is fulfilled in your hearing." And as we well know, Jesus went about performing many miracles. What I would like to draw your attention to is there came a time that after performing many of these miracles, Jesus asked the recipients not to tell anyone. The reason for this is that He knew the religious leaders were extremely offended and filled with hatred for Him and thereby wanted to get rid of Him. But the time for that had not been released yet, as Jesus had yet to receive the anointing for His crucifixion. This wasn't to happen until He had gone through the oil press on the Mount of Olives in the garden of Gethsemane releasing the anointing oil for the very thing He was born for. Also note that Jesus said the prophecy was fulfilled that day, when He was thirty years old, not on the day He was born, despite being born "the anointed one" as stated in the names given Jesus, being Christ, the Greek word, and Messiah, the Aramaic word, both of which mean "anointed one." Jesus is the 'Anointed

One" of the Father, chosen to bring salvation to the world. Thank you, Father God!

One more point I wanted to bring out through this is that some religious teachers have taught that the gift of the Holy Spirit, whom the oil is also representative of, is fully given to us when we receive the Baptism of the Holy Spirit, and therefore we should not desire nor seek God for "more anointing" or "more oil" because we already have been given it in full. They teach that the Holy Spirit does not come in parts, portions, or doses. Although this is true, what they have lacked in understanding is that there are seasons and times when God releases the oil or anointing for different levels of ministry that He calls us to as we grow and mature in Him and that the growing and maturing are extremely important as we have just learned.

This misconception can lead to many called of God to fall in disgrace, for it causes a zeal without knowledge to rise up within them and as they proceed, they end up in failure. Although the Scriptures teach us that zeal for God is an incredible force in this world for God's good plans, if zeal is not coupled with knowledge and understanding, it can cause us to be passionate without direction, without the guidance of the Holy Spirit, leading to missteps along our Spiritual journey. In order for our zeal to be rooted and grounded in truth, we must continually seek God through prayer for knowledge and through reading the Bible, through wise counsel and in seeking Him for direction. Romans 10:2-3 NKJV says – For I bear them witness that they have a zeal for God, but not according to knowledge. For they being ignorant of God's righteousness, and seeking to establish their own righteousness, have not submitted to the righteousness of God. And Proverbs 19:2 NLT declares – Enthusiasm without knowledge is no good; haste makes mistakes.

One last point on the "more oil" in the lamp is that it also represents more saints coming into the fold, coming into the Kingdom of God as the harvest is being reaped. And this brings us back to the last segment of the continuing vision. Remember at one point in it, my attention was drawn down onto the road by the sidewalk. It was as if I was supposed to perceive what season it was, because that also was of great importance here. I detected that it was very damp as the sidewalk and road were wet. My eyes shifted back to the sidewalk and edge of the road. Upon them were fallen leaves in varying shades of reds, yellows, and oranges. So, I looked up to the trees lining the sidewalk and road, and indeed, all of the leaves had changed into their fall colors. It was the fall season and what is of great relevance about the fall season, is that it is the season for harvest.

As I contemplated the meaning of this, I was led to John chapter 4:35-38 and heard in the Spirit that this is a "now time" word, a divine appointment time. Let's look at the verses in in the NLT version of the Bible. It reads – "You know the saying, 'Four months between planting and harvest.' But I say, wake up and look around. The fields are already ripe for harvest. The harvesters are paid good wages, and the fruit they harvest is people brought to eternal life. What joy awaits both the planter and the harvester alike! You know the saying, 'One plants and another harvests.' And it's true. I sent you to harvest where you didn't plant; others had already done the work, and now you will get to gather the harvest." As we learned earlier in this chapter, through all of the pressure on the earth as God uses the enemy as an oil press, putting pressure on people throughout the earth, He is ripening so many people's hearts to be harvested into His Kingdom. May we walk in the Spirit, being sensitive to Him as He leads us to those fertile fields He has prepared. Amen!

I was given another vision. It was of a door at our church bursting open as water, the color blue of the ocean waters in Miami, came gushing in. I wondered to myself what this meant knowing that large waters often indicated a sea of people, but instantly knew in my spirit that this isn't what the Spirit was showing me. Then I heard, "When the enemy comes in like a flood, the Spirit of the Lord will lift up a standard against him." I knew that a standard was also another name for a banner or a flag like when God instructed the tribes of Isreal in the Book of Numbers to set up camp around the Tent of Meeting in the wilderness according to their tribes, each with their own standard, flag, or banner. I personally conjure up in my mind battlefields of medieval times where they marched out to war with a flagbearer leading the way when I think of banners being lifted up. As I was thinking that, I then saw in my vision, a white horse and upon it sat a man in battle armor so pure, it appeared white. In his hand was a white banner with gold lettering I could not read, waving as he rode. Behind him was a countless army of other white horses following him with the riders all in snowy white robes.

At this, I instantly thought of the Scripture in Revelation 19 where Jesus sat on a white horse and the armies of heaven also sat on white horses dressed in clean, fine white linen and followed Him. As soon as I had made that connection, the wind blew the white flag in my vision and it was then I saw the words written in gold on the backside of it. It said, In Your Face! I had to chuckle at God's sense of humor. It was at this moment that I knew the Holy Spirit was conveying that even though God is allowing the enemy to run amuck throughout the world, using him as an oil press for His good purposes, that no matter what, He was still in control and the gates of Hell would not prevail against the church, the saints of God, and we together will have total victory. So, there's no reason to be intimidated by what we see going on in the earth with the naked eye! In short, we win!! So be courageous in all that you are called to do! Thank you, Father God!

CHAPTER EIGHT

GOD HAS A MASTER PLAN

The Bible in its entirety, from the Book of Genesis through the Book of Revelation shows us that God surely has a master plan. We can look at the prophecies of the Old Testament prophets and the prophecies fulfilled, as well as those spoken and yet to be fulfilled in the New Testament, and see this is so. However, God Himself tells us in Isaiah 55:8-9 NLT – "My thoughts are nothing like your thoughts," says the LORD. "And My ways are far beyond anything you could imagine. For just as the heavens are higher than the earth, so My ways are higher than your ways and My thoughts than your thoughts." Then in Romans 11:33-35, we find – Oh the depth of the riches both of the wisdom and knowledge of God! How unsearchable are His judgements and His ways past finding out! "For who has known the mind of the LORD? Or who has become His counselor? Or who has first given to Him and it shall be repaid to him?" As well as 1 Corinthians 2:9 – But as it is written: "Eye has not seen, nor ear heard, Nor have entered into the heart of man the things which God has prepared for those who love Him" We can only know the parts of His plans that He reveals to us as verse 16 declares – For "who has known the mind of the LORD that he may instruct Him?" But we have the mind of Christ.

There is one outstanding and incredible thing we can be confident of, and that is God's grand design, His master plan, was meant to include mankind, to include each and every one of us. In the beginning when God was creating everything, He didn't rest from His work until He had created man and woman, male and female, in His own image. Then God blessed them and said, "Be fruitful and multiply. Fill the earth and govern it. Reign over the fish in the sea, the birds in the sky, and all the animals that scurry along the ground." Every day that God created a part of His total creation, He called it good. But it wasn't until He had created man and woman, that He looked upon everything and called it very good. Thank you, Father!

So now, let's explore the plans He has for us, the plans He reveals to us through His holy Scriptures. Jeremiah 29:11 – For I know the thoughts that I think toward you, says the LORD, thoughts of peace and not of evil, to give you a future and a hope. We find in Romans 8:28 – And we know that all things work together for good to those who love God, to those who are called according to His purpose. What we learn from these two Scriptures is that in our journey here on earth, we can know and be encouraged that God is working something beautiful within us even if and when we cannot see it. And that we can rely on God to direct us to make the correct choices in our lives as we seek Him through prayer, Scripture, and Godly counsel. Then we receive clarity and direction and the more we seek Him, the clearer our path becomes.

We also learn that God wants us to become like Him. 1 John 3:1-2 reads – Behold what manner of love the Father has bestowed on us, that we should be called the sons of God! Therefore the world does not know us, because it did not know Him. Beloved, now we are children of God; and it has not yet been revealed what we shall be, but we know that when He is revealed, we shall be like Him, for we shall see Him as He is. He also desires to give us the same glory He has. Philippians 3:21 – who will transform our lowly body that it may be conformed to His glorious body, according to the working by which He is able even to subdue all things to Himself. God also plans to share everything with us. Revelation 21:7 – "He who overcomes shall inherit all things, and I will be his God and he shall be My son. God wants to share all things, nothing excluded, with us. Hebrews 2:8 – "You have put all things in subjection under His feet." For in that He put all in subjection under Him, He left nothing that is not put under Him. But now we do not yet see all things put under Him. And that's where we come in. Part of God's good plans for us is to share in putting all things under His feet in subjection to Him. Wow!

At this point, God brought to my remembrance a conversation we had not too long ago. I had been listening to a song on Christian radio and part of it was, "I know it's not much, but I've nothing else fit for a King except a heart singing hallelujah." Upon hearing this, my mind went to the Christmas special Little Drummer Boy and the song within it that says – our finest gifts we bring to lay before the King…I'm a poor boy, I have no gift to bring." It was then I heard the Holy Spirit speak. He said, "A heart full of hallelujah is not the greatest gift to give to the King. Yes, I absolutely want your heart, but that is only the beginning. I want all of you, body, soul, and spirit. The greatest gift you can give to the King is allowing Me to work in your life, allowing Me to mold, form, fashion, and mature you into the person I designed and created you to be, going forth and doing all that I purposed and created you to do, in Me." Thank you, Father! And I say, yes, Lord, all of me is yours!

In acknowledging what He wants of us, and determining to give that greatest gift to the King, let's look again at Hebrews 2:8 – "You have put all things in subjection under His feet." For in that He put all in subjection under Him, He left nothing that is not put under Him. But now we do not yet see all things put under Him. In this, we should see that God has put everything under our feet. When we acknowledge this truth, and desire His desire for us, we can submit ourselves to His plan in our lives. We can surrender our desires, our fears, and doubts to Him, knowing that He is in complete control. I find it intriguing that this Scripture aligns with what is written in Psalm 8:6, where it's declared that man is made a little lower than the angels and put in charge of the works of God's hands. This emphasizes the value God places on us and celebrates His creative work while praising Him for using humans, including you and me, to rule His creation! Through prayer, praise and worship, and obedience to His Word, we demonstrate His sovereignty in the earth. We reveal that we do believe in His power and wisdom by seeking His will in all areas of our lives and trusting in His guidance. Letting go of our own plans and surrendering to God's will is inviting His presence to work in and through us, aligning ourselves to His purpose and master plan for our lives. Let us therefore develop a deep-seated trust in His authority over all things. We can grab hold of and totally rely on His complete dominion whether we are wrestling with personal trials, world-wide upheavals like we see happening right now, or spiritual battles. Living in unwavering confidence and peace, knowing that Jesus governs all things, we can navigate life's challenges with assurance and hope, and we can give the greatest gift to our King!

I know it can appear extremely daunting to think of becoming what God created us to be and even more so in doing what He created us to do. However, when we recognize that God's plan for our lives is not built upon our own personal strengths or by what we can achieve, but by His strength and our faith to submit to it, it eases any pressure that we put on our own selves. Faith and trust are wonderful things! They help us realize that our purpose in life is intricately woven into God's grand design, His master plan. We are created in His image and filled with God-given unique talents, giftings, and passions. Recognizing our identity as beloved men and women of God gives us a firm foundation to stand on. Knowing who we are in Christ allows us to step confidently into the roles that He has called and chosen for us to fulfill. Each and every one of us have a special purpose that only we can contribute to His plan. When He leads us to discover and recognize these gifts and calling, we grow closer to Him understanding our place in His divine purposes and plans, causing us to yield more and more of ourselves to Him, crying out, "Yes, Lord!"

Let's read Psalm 139:13-16 NKJV – For you formed my inward parts; You covered me in my mother's womb. I will praise You, for I am fearfully and wonderfully made; Marvelous are Your works, And that my soul knows very well. My frame was not hidden from You, When I was made in secret, And skillfully wrought in the lowest parts of the earth, Your eyes saw my substance, being yet unformed. And in Your book they are all written, The days fashioned for me, When as yet there were none of them. And at the NLT version. – You made all the delicate, inner parts of my body and knit me together in my mother's womb. Thank you for making me so wonderfully complex! Your workmanship is marvelous—how well I know it. You watched me as I was being formed in utter seclusion, as I was woven together in the dark of the womb. You saw me before I was born. Every day of my life was recorded in your book. Every moment was laid out before a single day had passed.

And now let's read Ephesians 2:10 NKJV – For we are His workmanship, created in Christ Jesus for good works, which God prepared beforehand that we should walk in them. And again, at the NLT version – For we are God's masterpiece. He has created us anew in Christ Jesus, so we can do the good things He planned for us long ago. When we grasp exactly what God is telling us through these passages of Scripture, we should be energized, encouraged, empowered, courageous, and confident. We should experience faith arising strong and sure within us. Let's break this down. God is telling us that not only did He skillfully weave us, create us intricately, every single fiber of our being, knowing us before we were even born, but He also fashioned the days we would live in and had written our story out in His book. Every single day of our life was recorded in His book, every single moment was laid out beforehand, before one single day had passed! We are His workmanship, created in Jesus for good works that God planned for us beforehand, planned out for us long ago! Let me repeat that. We are God's handiwork, His masterpiece, created in Christ Jesus to do the good works that God prepared in advance for us to do every single day! When we can wrap our brains around what God is saying to us, when we grasp the meaning of what He said, BOOM! We understand that He's made the way and all we are responsible for is yielding ourselves, body, soul, and spirit to Him and walk that path specifically fashioned for us in faith, allowing Him to have His way in our lives! No pressure, just surrender, because He prepared all of it in advance for us! Wow! Thank you, Father!

Also, when we comprehend what God revealed above, we can see why we shouldn't be anxious for things in this life and should as Philippians 4:6-7 NLT says – Don't worry about anything; instead pray about everything. Tell God what you need, and thank Him for all He has done. Then you will experience God's peace, which exceeds anything we can understand. His peace will guard your hearts and minds as you live in Christ Jesus. And Jesus Himself said in Matthew 6:25-26 NKJV – "Therefore I say to you, do not worry about your life, what you will eat or what you will drink; nor about your body, what you will put on. Is not life more than food and the body more than clothing? Look at the birds of the air, for they neither sow nor reap nor gather into barns; yet your heavenly Father feeds them. Are you not of more value than they?"

I can personally attest to God caring for the creatures He created, watching over them, and seeing they have food and shelter and are taken care of and His promise to take care of our needs according to His riches in glory. I have a real-life story that confirms both. A few years ago, my husband Bill and I were standing out in the backyard one summer day, basking in the warming rays of the sun and admiring the beauty of all of the different flowers thriving in our flower beds and gardens. Suddenly, a chipmunk ran past us, continued to the house, and dove into a hole it had burrowed at the foundation. As a matter of fact, many chipmunks had dug these holes both along the front and back of the house. This really concerned Bill because he said they were undermining the foundation of our home. He then said to me, "You know, if we had a cat, we wouldn't have all of these rodents rampantly running around our property wreaking havoc." I just looked at him, nodded my head in acknowledgment, and went back to soaking up some sunshine.

Fast forward a few days later and the heat was on. It was a super humid day, you know, the kind where you stick to everything you lean against, sit on, and anything your body touches. The kind of day you perspire without even lifting a finger or exerting your body in any way, shape, or form. The kind of day everybody either flocks to the beach, spend their day in their pools, or stay inside in the air conditioning. The weathermen on the news were forecasting severe thunderstorms for later in the evening. And sure enough, as evening fell, we were issued a severe thunderstorm watch. Not long after that, it was upgraded to a severe thunderstorm warning, and not long after that, lightening flashed across the skies making it appear as daylight. The lightening was accompanied by big crashes of thunder that shook the whole house and rattled the windows. In the thick of the storm, Bill heard a large crack and was sure a large branch had fallen from one of the big Maple trees in the backyard. He was hoping it hadn't done any damage to the patio, sidewalk, or anything else for that matter.

So, after the storm had passed, he went out into the garage to the back door to see if there was indeed a branch down. When he opened the back door and stepped out, he spotted bright glowing eyes up on the bench of the back deck. He then heard a meow. When he looked closer, he saw a pitiful looking kitty sitting there in the dark. As his eyes looked further out into the yard, he saw three more sets of glowing eyes all around the deck that belonged to what he thinks was a possum, a raccoon, and the other, he wasn't quite sure about. He believed they were after the kitty.

At that point, the skinny little kitty jumped down from the deck, ran up to him and started rubbing on his legs. He then stepped back inside the garage and called for me. He told me to go look out the large back window in the kitchen and when I did, the poor scrawny kitty dashed over to the house below the window, put her feet up on the siding of the house, looked right at me into my eyes, and began crying, meowing loudly. That was it. It was all over. She was mine now. I went outside, picked her up and took her inside. Poor thing had no collar and was skeletal. It was obvious someone had dumped her a while ago and she had been all alone fending for herself as best she could. But being in the woods behind our house was getting the best of her. I named her Lacey and she acclimated to us quite well. She loved spending her days outside hunting down and catching chipmunk after chipmunk. Bill commented several times that she was most certainly earning her keep. What a good, good Father we have. He heard Bill's lament about the chipmunks and needing a cat, and watched over Lacey, directing her to a home where she was needed and would be wanted and well taken care of. He met two needs at once for He cares for every creature and cares about what we care about.

In seeing that our God is in every little detail of our lives, and in seeing how much He cares for us from the smallest of things to the enormous looming things in our lives, let us set aside every single thing that would hinder us from fully seeking and submitting our entire lives to Him. Let us cast down every lie the enemy whispers in our ears trying to cause doubt to rear its ugly head. Let's ignore all the shiny distractions placed in our paths trying to lure us away from fulfilling the plans God has for us. Let us set aside the things we give more attention to in our lives than our Bible studies and personal time spent with Him in prayer. Let us not allow the troubles of the world infiltrate and rob us of our God-given peace. Let us rededicate ourselves to Him as when we first believed. Let us set aside our bad habits and/or anything and everything that tries to pull us away from our faith. Let us set aside anything that desires to entangle us and slow us down in our spiritual journey.

Let's do as Paul encourages in Hebrews 12 and strip off every weight that slows us down, especially the sin that so easily trips us up. And let us run with endurance the race God has set before us. We do this by keeping our eyes on Jesus, the champion who initiates and perfects our faith. Because of the joy awaiting Him, He endured the cross, disregarding its shame. Now He is seated in the place of honor beside God's throne. Think of all of the hostility He endured from sinful people; then you won't become weary and give up. After all, you have not yet given your lives in your struggle against sin.

Let us remember that God has prepared the way for us even before time began, and that He set us up with everything we could possibly need to succeed in the very thing He created us for. Let us go forth in confidence and give Him the greatest gift we can give to our King. Let us do all of this by saying one simple but powerful word to Him. Let us answer His call and simply say, yes! Yes to His master plan not only for our own lives, but for His entire eternal plan and our role in it. Then prepare to be amazed, blessed, and have our minds completely boggled at what good things He does in and through our lives. Amen!

CHAPTER NINE

THE ANCIENT OF DAYS

God has many names sprinkled throughout the Scriptures, each describing a facet of His character, revealing yet another attribute of who He is. In the Book of Genesis alone, I quickly found seven of them. Elohim meaning God, Creator, Mighty One. El Shaddai meaning God Almighty, All Sufficient One. El Elyon meaning God Most High. Adonai meaning Lord, Master. El Olam meaning The Everlasting God. Jehovah Jireh meaning The LORD will Provide. And El Roi meaning The God Who Sees Me. In the Book of Exodus, I found Yahweh -YHWH meaning I AM WHO I AM. Jehovah Rapha meaning The LORD Who Heals. Jehovah Nissi meaning The LORD Is My Banner. El Gibhor meaning The Mighty God and El Chuwl meaning The God Who Gave You Birth, the last two both found in the Book of Isaiah. Also, we find Jehovah Shalom in the Book of Judges meaning The LORD Is Peace. We find in the Book of 1 Samuel Jehovah Sabaoth meaning The LORD of Hosts. In the Book of Jeremiah, we find Jehovah Tsidkenu meaning The LORD Our Righteousness. We find Immanuel in the Book of Matthew meaning God with us. This is not an exhaustive compilation of His names, however, does include some key ones.

What I want to focus on in this chapter, however, is the name Ancient of Days only found in the Book of Daniel and used three times because it is the name God gave me to use when I was seeking Him as to what I should refer to Him by as the One giving me the continuing visions at the beginning of this book. He clearly spoke, saying, "Refer to Me as the Ancient of Days." And so I did, not quite knowing what He would be revealing throughout this book. Let's now explore what He wants to unveil about Himself as the Ancient of Days.

The first time the Ancient of Days is mentioned is in Daniel 7:9. Let's start from there as Daniel describes what He saw in the vision given him and read through verse 10. – "I watched till thrones were put in place, And the Ancient of Days was seated; His garment was white as snow, And the hair of His Head was like pure wool. His throne was a fiery flame, Its wheels a burning fire; A fiery stream issued And came forth from before Him. A thousand thousands ministered to Him; Ten thousand times ten thousand stood before Him. The court was seated, And the books were opened." The title Ancient of Days underlines God's eternal nature. Unlike we humans, who are restricted by time, God exists outside of time and has no beginning or end. We can find this confirmed in other Scripture such as Psalm 90:2 that states – Before the mountains were brought forth, or ever You had formed the earth and the world, even everlasting to everlasting, You are God. Revelation 1:8 – "I am the Alpha and Omega, the First and the Last…"

Let's next look at the significance of the imagery presented to Daniel. His white garment and woolen white hair emphasize His holiness, purity, and righteousness. His hair being as white as wool also represents His perfect wisdom. As the Ancient of Days, He is the source of all knowledge and understanding. We can find this reiterated in Proverbs 3:19 – The LORD by wisdom founded the earth; by understanding He established the heavens. His fiery throne demonstrates His consuming power and authority, the fire representing the searching judgment no evil can resist, like Deuteronomy 4:24 states. – "For the Lord your God is a consuming fire, a jealous God." And yet, He purifies those He receives like what's found in Isaiah 1:18 – "Come now, and let us reason together," Says the LORD, "Though your sins are like scarlet, They shall be as white as snow; Though they are red like crimson, they shall be as wool."

The throne/chariot imagery echoes other Scripture of visions given like Ezekiel 1:26-28 – And above the firmament over their heads was the likeness of a throne, in appearance like a sapphire stone; on the likeness of the throne was a likeness with the appearance of a man high above it. Also from the appearance of His waist and upward I saw, as it were, the color of amber with the appearance of fire all around within it; and from the appearance of His waist downward I saw, as it were, the appearance of fire with brightness all around. Like the appearance of a rainbow in a cloud on a rainy day, so was the appearance of the brightness all around it. This was the appearance of the likeness of the glory of the Lord. Also, the fiery throne and the opening of the books portray God as the righteous judge.

The Ancient of Days evaluates the deeds of all mankind and renders judgement with perfect justice just as Psalm 11:7 declares – For the LORD is righteous, He loves righteousness; His countenance beholds the upright. And the thousands ministering to Him symbolizes His majesty and all-encompassing dominion, His supreme authority over all creation. As sovereign ruler, His dominion is unshakable as well as eternal. This is also found in Psalm 103:13 – The LORD has established His throne in heaven, and His kingdom rules over all. And Hebrews 12:28-29 – Therefore, since we are receiving a kingdom which cannot be shaken, let us have grace, by which we may serve God acceptably with reverence and godly fear. For our God is a consuming fire.

The second time Ancient of Days is mentioned is in Daniel 7:13-14. It reads – I was watching in the night visions, And behold, One like the Son of Man, Coming with the clouds of heaven! He came to the Ancient of Days, And they brought Him near before Him. Then to Him was given dominion and glory and a kingdom, That all peoples, nations, and languages should serve Him. His dominion is an everlasting dominion, Which shall not pass away, And His kingdom the one Which shall not be destroyed. Here in the courtroom, we see the Ancient of Days giving the Son of Man, a name Jesus often referred to Himself as, dominion, glory, and a kingdom after riding in on the clouds of heaven. This signifies that Jesus shares in the divine authority of the Father, and aligns with Jesus' teaching about His exalted position in Matthew 28:18 – And Jesus came and spoke to them, Saying, "All authority has been given Me in heaven and on earth." It also speaks to Jesus' alluding to Daniel's vision while explaining about His coming in Mark 13:26 – "Then they will see the Son of Man coming in the clouds with great power and authority."

So, Jesus, who was both fully human and fully God, arrived on the clouds, which is a mode of transportation reserved for God when He comes to save or to judge. Psalm 68:4 – Sing to God, sing praises to His name; Extol Him who rides on the clouds…and Isaiah 19:1 – Behold, the LORD rides on a swift cloud, And will come into Egypt; The idols of Egypt will totter at His presence, And the heart of Egypt will melt in its midst. – Then was given full authority, dominion, glory, and the kingdom. The New Testament mirrors this imagery in John's vision of the risen Christ. Revelation 1:14-15 – His head and hair were white like wool, as white as snow, and His eyes like a flame of fire; His feet were like fine brass, as if refined in a furnace, and His voice as the sound of many waters…This perfectly coincides with the Daniel 7:13-14 above. Continuing in Revelation 1:17-18 we find Jesus identified Himself as "the First and the Last" a title the Lord uses in Isaiah 44:6 – "Thus says the LORD, the King of Israel, And his Redeemer, the LORD of hosts: 'I am the First and I am the Last; Besides Me there is no God' and claims the keys of death and hades, sovereign over life and judgement. This transfer is the Son's sharing the Ancient of Day's divine nature and remaining a distinct person who in Daniel's vision receives the Kingdom from the Ancient of Days.

The final time the Ancient of Days appears, is in Daniel 7:22 – …the Ancient of Days came, and a judgement was made in favor of the saints of the Most High. And the time came for the saints to possess the kingdom. Hallelujah! The Ancient of Days presides over a court where justice is rendered. This is the assurance we have that God will right every wrong and vindicate us, His people. 2 Corinthians 5:10 – For we must all appear before the judgement seat of Christ, that each one may receive the things done in the body, according to what he has done, whether good or bad. In a world filled with chaos, riots, hatred, division, and uncertainty, as seen through our human eyes, we can rest assured the Ancient of Days is in control and guarantees that evil will not have the final word! Our God reigns! Revelation 11:5 – The kingdoms of this world have become the kingdom of our Lord and His Christ, and He shall reign forever and ever! Let us know that court is in session and the books are open. This is on ongoing session until all that the Ancient of

Days has planned is complete and He fulfills His plans for the earth. The books won't be complete until then, but know that your name will be in them. And the best part is that you get to choose if you're on the winning or losing side, whether the Judge rules in your favor or not. Thank you, Father!

It's quite interesting to me that people in the past, on up to the present, keep trying to erase history when it pertains to God. I'm not sure why they do this, but perhaps one reason is they think that if they can erase it, then heaven's courtroom won't be in session and judgement won't be rendered, and therefore they can, if they're in leadership roles, keep their own ideologies and therefore, power. Perhaps some want to live by the ostrich's plan of action being, stick your head in the sand because if you can't see it, then it really isn't there. I look at that as being willfully ignorant just like the people of Noah's day. However, whatever the reason, it's been happening since Biblical times. Before we get into some examples, I want to declare that it will never happen, God's word is eternal and is unaffected by the changing tides of life and I can say this in complete confidence because Scripture tells us so. Psalm 119:89 declares – Forever, O LORD, Your word is settled in heaven. Isaiah 40:8 decrees – The grass withers, the flower fades, But the word of our God stands forever. And Isaiah 55:11 – So shall My word be that goes forth from My mouth; It shall not return to me void, But it shall accomplish what I please, And it shall prosper in the thing for which I sent it. Matthew 24:35 – Heaven and earth shall pass away but My words will by no means pass away.

The first example found in the Scriptures of men trying to stop and thereby erase God's word is found in Jeremiah chapter 3, verses 1-32. Within we find that the prophet Jeremiah received from God a command to deliver a potent indictment of the sinful people of Judah. His secretary, Baruch wrote the words down in a scroll which condemned the transgressions prevalent all throughout Judah and warned of Jerusalem's destruction unless they repented. When King Jehoiakim heard the reading, he found it highly offensive and lashed out by slicing the scroll to pieces and burning it section by section. This shows his lack of any reverential fear that would lead to repentance. Instead, he thought he could erase God's message by burning the scroll.

Next, Jeremiah received another command of God to rewrite every single word on a new scroll and include direct additional warnings for the king. We find this in verses 28-31 – Take yet another scroll, and write on it all the former words that were in the first scroll which Jehoiakim the king of Judah has burned. And you shall say to Jehoiakim the king of Judah, "Thus says the LORD: "You have burned this scroll, saying, 'Why have you written in it that the king of Babylon will certainly come and destroy this land and cause man and beast to cease from here?'" "Therefore thus says the LORD concerning Jehoiakim king of Judah: He shall have no one to sit on the throne of David, and his dead body shall be cast out to the heat of the day and the frost of the night. I will punish him, his family, and his servants for their iniquity; and I will bring on them, on the inhabitants of Jerusalem, and on the men of Judah all the doom that I have pronounced against them; but they did not heed." We can see that God did preserve His words for we read them here in the book of Jeremiah. And eventually, the message the king so despised came to pass when the Babylonians destroyed Jerusalem and took into exile many Judeans.

A couple more examples from the Bible is when King Herod wished to kill Jesus, the newborn King of the Jews and therefore slaughtered every male child two years old and under in Bethlehem found in Matthew 2:16 and of course he failed as God had warned Joseph in a dream to take the child and flee to Egypt. Then, of course, the most well-known event when the religious leaders determined to kill Jesus and shut Him up. However, they played right into the plans of God and here we are today with our Holy Bibles! If you know church history at all, then you also know that Antiochus Epiphanes desecrated the temple in Jerusalem, set up an altar to Zeus on top of the altar to God. He then banned all outward appearances of obeying the laws such as observing the Sabbath and circumcision and threatened the death penalty for anyone found observing. He also hunted down and burned copies of the Hebrew Scriptures. But the people became even more determined to preserve and protect them and hid them, refusing to surrender them. This eventually died down and here we are today, reading the Word of God! Also, in Christian history we learn about Emperor Diocletan writing edicts to dismantle Christian worship by ordering the burning of all Christiam worship places and the destruction of all copies of the Scriptures. What followed was a horrible persecution of the Christian people. But here we are today, studying our Holy Bibles! On top of that, in our modern day, we also have electronic devices to read the Scriptures, online libraries, and mobile apps that offer free copies of Scripture in a slew of different languages! Our God's Word will not be abolished!

One falsehood I'd like to address is the schools trying to wipe out the truth of God about our founding fathers of this great country, the United Staes of America. The thing being taught at some schools and spread around via some political arenas is that our founding fathers were a bunch of old racist white men. Wrong! In actuality, our founding fathers were young men of faith, and our country was founded on the principles of God. The men varied in their beliefs but none-the-less were men of faith. Therefore, religion played a significant role shaping political ideologies, governance, human rights, and faith in the public arena. Let's take a look at some of these young men. We have George Washington who believed that faith was essential for morality and civic virtue. He often publicly touted the importance of religion in public society. We have Thomas Jefferson whose beliefs led him to advocate for religious freedom and famously wrote about the wall of separation between church and state. We also have John Adams who believed a religious and moral people were necessary for a successful republic. He often spoke about the importance of virtue and morality in governing. Next, we have Benjamin Franklin whose religious views influenced his belief in the importance of education and civic responsibility. As a matter of fact, he founded the University of Pennsylvania to encourage these values. I'll mention just one more and that's James Madison. His religious beliefs are what influenced, and why he so strongly advocated for, the separation of church and state. He firmly believed that government should not interfere in religious practices at all! Our Lord's word will not be annihilated or covered up! It will never pass away! He makes sure of it as He watches over it and makes sure it flourishes! Mankind will never be successful in erasing God's Word, as we've gone over, nor history because as my pastor loves to teach, history is HIS-story.

There is one more thing I'd like to discuss and that is, in more recent history, we have the Supreme Court's rulings on cases of prayer in public schools going on since the 1950s and 1960s. There have been six court cases since then with the most well-known one in 1962, Engle vs Vitale. This case is where a New York school district's decision to have students say a prayer aloud at the start of each school day was challenged by the parents of ten students in the district. The Supreme Court found the school was violating the Establishment Clause in the First Amendment that prohibits congress from establishing a religion. The case specifically addressed whether a school district could create an officially approved prayer. This is the case most often referred to as the one that banned prayer from schools. However, the one I want to discuss is the case Lee vs Weisman in 1992. In this case, a middle school was challenged on the grounds of inviting a clergyman to offer an opening invocation and a closing benediction at a graduation ceremony. With a 5-4 vote, the Supreme Court ruled that such practices violate the First Amendment. The reason I want to talk about this one is because of two words. Graduation Ceremony. You see, I can share a testimony proving that God shows up when asked upon regardless of what man says and He assures His word does not die!

The year was 2002, and my first-born daughter, Brooke, was Salutatorian of her graduating class. She loved God, prayer, her school, her friends, and her youth group. She had a deep desire within her heart to pray over her classmates before she gave her speech, however, she had been told she could not pray in a public school. A moment of silence could be offered, but would be offered by someone else, a school official, in the opening of the ceremony. But Brooke had this tug in her heart that just would not let her go. So, the next time she had Master's Commission through her youth group, she went and spoke with her youth pastor about it and He knew the law regarding it, inside and out, and shared it with Brooke. After that, a plan was formed that included her best friend, fellow classmate, and fellow youth group member.

The night of the graduation ceremony, the auditorium was packed to full capacity. When Brooke was announced as Salutatorian and asked to come forward to give her speech, she walked up to the podium with such confidence and poise, any parent would be proud, but none more than her dad and I. Once she adjusted the microphone, she began to speak. She said, "The first thing I would like to do is to call up Danielle to pray," and Danielle came forward. There was complete silence in the place. Danielle prayed diligently over her fellow classmates and graduates. She prayed the word of God and blessings over them all. She then handed over the microphone back to Brooke who proceeded to give her speech. When Brooke was finished, she was greeted with immense applause! Dr. Green, the school superintendent spoke next. With a big smile on his face, he announced that it would take the Salutatorian of the class to search out a legal way to have prayer, speak the word of God, over her classmates. And the whole graduating class erupted in a standing ovation complete with cheers, whoops, whistles, and applause. You see, the law pertaining to student prayer at graduation ceremonies was that the graduating speaker could not pray, and could not invite any clergy to come and pray, however, could invite up a fellow student to pray. I believe God desires for all of us to search out matters pertaining to Him and His Word and as we do, He will lead us into His wisdom and His knowledge and His divine guidance. He watches over it to make sure it performs the very thing He sent it for in every situation. To God, the Ancient of Days, be all the glory, forever and ever, amen!

CHAPTER TEN

THE TIME IS NOW

The Lord gave me another vision while I was in Saturday morning prayer at church, the final vision for this book. I saw before me a mountainous range across the horizon. The mountains were of different varying heights with one in the center being somewhat higher than the others. The mountains weren't in a straight line, but had depth to them indicating they were covering a lot of area and that this mountainscape was quite expansive. This scene was set in dull skies, comparable to dusk, not as bright as the noonday, but not as dark as the midnight hour. It was something in between. As I was studying the scene before me, I saw a dark, smokey black, cloudlike form slowly arising from the earth between some of the mountains, just to the left of the tallest one. It sometimes was slowly twirling and churning like a black mist but then would change shape into what I could best describe as an enormous apelike beast, then return to churning, then into the beastly form again. As I was watching this, I heard a voice from heaven which I recognized as the voice of the Ancient of Days, ask me what I saw. After I described what I saw rising up from the earth, just as I have for you here, the voice said, "Yes, and it is earthly and sensual!"

At that point, I saw the rising, inky, ominous, whirling formation hit a plateau, an invisible ceiling, and begin spreading out in all directions as it could rise no higher. It then began to drop a very fine obsidian dustlike silt over everything, causing the atmosphere to become all the more darkened. I heard the Spirit of God tell me to look up and at that moment, I was able to see above the ceiling of blackness in the sky, and what I saw was mesmerizing. In the sky over the darkness, there were countless dazzling, vibrantly twinkling, gemlike heavenly bodies in all sorts of fantastic colors, more brilliant than any colors I've ever seen before. What I was being shown reminded me of some pictures of galaxies and stars captured by the Hubble Telescope way out in space, except these were flashing so beautifully and had no restricting boundaries or ceiling. They reached higher than can be measured with the naked eye.

Suddenly, my vision shifted back down to the black silt falling and the voice again asked me, "What do you see?" I described to Him the black, powdery, silty dust falling to the ground, as I described it above. Then the voice of God spoke, sounding so heartbroken, "Look how it lulls them into sleep and slumber." It's rather hard to explain, but I was able to feel within my own being, the pain within His voice as He spoke and it made my eyes well up with tears. It was then that I noticed some people walking about aimlessly, as in a daze, wandering and meandering around, not aware of their surroundings and other people curled up in fetal positions, in a deep, heavy sleep with the raven black, powdery, sediment still falling upon and enshrouding them. As I was gloomily gazing upon them, feeling brokenhearted along with Him, I noticed some bright lights appearing in my peripheral vision. My focus was then honed in on those intense forward moving lights. I then observed that those brilliant illuminations were large round globes being held in front of people's chests, their arms fully outstretched in front of them with hands touching, holding the spheres. The globes were extremely bright and reminded me of the new LED headlights on vehicles, but the remarkable thing was that they didn't blind me or sting and burn my eyes in the darkness like those headlights do.

My focus was then brought to the people holding the globes of light. They were marching like an army, moving closer and closer to the base of the tallest mountain. Also, I was able to perceive that this army of light bearers was coming from all directions, even though some were out of my view, behind the mountain. As they approached, the smaller mountains began to slowly move nearer and nearer to the highest one. In addition, as this marching army of people were gathering closer and closer together and closer and closer to the base of the largest mountain, it began to rain, not as in a storm, but as a fresh, pure spring rain, gentle, steady, and invigorating. As the rain fell, I saw the raindrops washing everything in my view clean, the shadowy, dusty silt was being eliminated from the air and absconded from everything it had previously covered, thus making everything pure and unpolluted.

Unexpectedly, something incredible began happening right before my eyes! Those glowing orbs of brilliant light being held close to the hearts of the army of people began changing. They were crackling with power and transforming into smaller versions of the heavenly bodies I previously viewed above the blackened atmosphere. They appeared alive and powerful and were swirling and sparkling in all of those splendid, vibrant colors, and resembling raw uncut gemstones inside mini galaxies. These were all within those globes which were now completely transparent. While I was watching in awestruck wonder, completely captivated by what was occurring before me, something even more impressive happened! These newly fashioned glowing orbs began to melt right into the chests and hearts of the multitude of persons, morphing them into those very heavenly bodied, living, uncut, gemstones in an array of colors I had never laid my eyes upon before.

Simultaneously, the other mountains from the mountainscape began merging into the one large mountain causing it to grow higher and higher, while at the same time, the people, turned living stones, were being placed into the mountain itself with unseen hands, as well as all of the heavenly bodied galaxy-like forms I originally saw above the darkness covering the earth. They were slowly flying into the mountainside and becoming part of it. While all of this was occurring, not only was the mountain growing to an unmeasurable height, but the base was expanding and increasing across the earth until it covered the whole earth which, in turn, became the mountain itself!

As I gazed at this miraculous and wonderous sight before me, the Ancient of Days spoke and instructed me to notice that all of the jewels and gems were melded together with no visible seams or metal-working that man would have had to use making jewelry, a mosaic, or a sculpture. He then spoke one last time and declared, "Tell them the time is now!" I instantly knew in my spirit, at that moment, God had given me this vision for the last chapter of this book He had called me to write.

While driving home after prayer, the two words the Spirit of the Lord had given me – earthly and sensual – kept running around in my mind and I kept repeating them aloud as I drove home. I knew there was a Scripture in the Bible that contained those two words in that exact order, but it wasn't directly coming to mind. So, upon arriving home, I immediately did some research and then grabbed my Bible. I turned to James, chapter 3 NKJV and began reading at verse 13 – Who is wise and understanding among you? Let him show by good conduct that his works are done in the meekness of wisdom. But if you have bitter envy and self-seeking in your hearts, do not boast and lie against the truth. This wisdom does not descend from above, but is earthly, sensual, demonic. – And there it was! Earthly, sensual, and demonic. In the KJV, it reads earthly, sensual, devilish. As my heart started beating faster, and goosebumps raised up on my arms, I continued, picking up at verse 16 and read through 17. – For where envy and self-seeking exist, confusion and every evil thing are there. But the wisdom that is from above is first pure, then peaceable, gentle, willing to yield, full of mercy and good fruits, without partiality and without hypocrisy. – As I read through those verses, so much of this vision began to make sense. It's like the interpretation of parts of it were just dropped into my spirit and completely blew my mind!

Let's start with the wisdom of the world. What the Ancient of Days shared with me was that the dark cloudlike form arising from the earth into the atmosphere, hitting a ceiling where it could rise no more, then slowly began covering the world and people on the earth in darkness, was earthly, sensual, devilish. The word earthly here indicates being rooted in "human" perceptions and experiences gleaned from one's emotions and moods, not from the guidance of God or the Holy Spirit.

Next, let's look at the word sensual. What this word narrates is people's main motivations being driven by emotions, but also carnal desires indicating that worldly wisdom is self-serving and merely temporary, not lasting. Seeking direction on any given matter based only upon one's own emotional reactions and feelings, leads to decision making that could be detrimental not only to oneself, but to other people as well, and can be characterized as self-seeking and not God seeking.

And lastly, let's take a deeper look into the word devilish/demonic. It shines a light on the very nature of this kind of wisdom. Worldly wisdom is influenced by forces that are contrary to the Word of God; influenced by the god of this world or the prince of the power of the air (which is why the darkness hit a ceiling in the vision), otherwise known as the devil and as demonic. It therefore falls short of God's righteousness and can spread like wildfire with the ashes causing conflict, strife, and ultimately, division among people as they are so completely self-absorbed. Therefore, it is vital that we be vigilant in seeking out the wisdom of God and guard ourselves from becoming entwined in the snares of the earthly, sensual, and devilish wisdom of this world.

A couple of corresponding Scripture passages can be found in Proverbs 3:5-7 – "Trust in the Lord with all your heart, and lean not to your own understanding; In all your ways acknowledge Him, And He shall direct your paths. Do not be wise in your own eyes; Fear the Lord and depart from evil." Also, from the New Testament, we have 1 Corinthians 3:18-19 – "Let no one deceive himself. If anyone among you seems to be wise in this age, let him become a fool that he may become wise. For the wisdom of this world is foolishness with God. For it is written, 'He catches the wise in their own craftiness,' and again, 'The Lord knows the thoughts of the wise, that they are futile.'"

As I contemplated on the darkness from the arising beastlike black cloud and its dark silty dust covering everything on the earth as representing the wisdom of the world, I remembered Isaiah 60:1-2 – "Arise, shine; For your light has come! And the glory of the Lord is risen upon you. For behold, the darkness shall cover the earth, And deep darkness the people; But the Lord will arise over you, And His glory will be seen upon you." This is a Messianic prophecy given to Isaiah foretelling the coming of Jesus Christ to the earth as the Messiah. But as discussed in a previous chapter, the whole Bible is prophetic in nature and therefore, a given prophecy can refer to something going on in the time the prophecy is given, but can also refer to an upcoming event and even more than one, as God brings us into maturity and reveals a deeper meaning. In the above vision, the Ancient of Days showed me the earth being covered in darkness, and deep darkness upon the people. Recall how He said to look at how the dirty, black, dark silt from the beastlike swirling cloud (now revealed as the wisdom of the world and from the devil) was covering some people and painfully spoke to how it lulled them to sleep and to slumber. 1Thessalonians 5:5-8 – "You are all sons of light and sons of the day. We are not of the night nor of darkness. Therefore let us not sleep, as others do, but let us watch and be sober. For those who sleep, sleep at night…"

What came next was a large army of people carrying a bright light. Let's now explore that and delve into what The Ancient of Days was revealing. In essence, all throughout the Holy Bible, light symbolizes God/Jesus, faith, and holiness. As the sons of God, we are not only to walk in the light, but be the light for others. There are numerous examples we could look at to confirm this, but I want to focus on the ones the Lord showed me pertaining to the vision He revealed. Matthew 4:16 NLT reads – "The people who sat in darkness have seen a great light, And for those who lived in the land where death casts its shadow, a light has shined." This was confirmation of the prophecy in Isaiah 9:1-2 about Jesus' coming, and Matthew, here, quotes it as the beginning of Jesus' ministry. However, it essentializes a potent message of hope for everyone from that point on. It underscores that even in the darkest of times, light, refreshing, and renewal are possible through faith.

Next, in John 8:12 Jesus declares – "I am the light of the world. He who follows me shall not walk in darkness, but have the light of life." Ephesians 5:8 – "For you were once darkness, but now you are light in the Lord. Walk as children of light." And lastly, from the Old Testament, Ecclesiastes 2:13 – … "Wisdom is better than foolishness just as light is better than darkness." So, the army of people in the vision were once walking in the wisdom of the world, but through faith in Jesus, the light, they now were soldiers for Jesus, carrying His light and were now light bearers themselves, walking in the wisdom of God.

In the vision, when the frontline of light bearers gathered together and were approaching the foot of the mountain, it began to rain. As I was pondering how I would describe the rain in the vision, I noticed then that the rain was as gentle and pure as a spring rain; fresh and cleansing, bringing forth new life after the long and dark winter. I recalled how in the Old Testament, the spring rain was called the "latter rain" in the lunar calendar they used. The latter rain was essential in maturing their crops which they planted in the fall, referred to as the "former rain" and I was wondering what God was showing me. He then spoke and said, "This rain represents My wisdom. Just as I, in My wisdom and knowledge, created the earth and the ways that I sustain it naturally, so I rain down My wisdom to sustain My sons and daughters who ask for it, spiritually. This is the time for My wisdom to abound in My people and it will rain down upon them when they ask. I will open up the windows of heaven and pour down blessings upon them." Wow!

I instantly thought of the Book of Isaiah, chapter 55, verses 8-11 NLT. It declares – "My thoughts are nothing like your thoughts," says the Lord. "And My ways are far beyond anything you could imagine. For just as the heavens are higher than the earth, so My ways are higher than your ways and My thoughts higher than your thoughts. The rain and snow come down from the heavens and stay on the ground to water the earth. They cause the grain to grow, producing seed for the farmer and bread for the hungry. It is the same with My word. I send it out, and it always produces fruit. It will accomplish all I want it to, and it will prosper everywhere I send it." As well as, Zechariah 10:1 NKJV – Ask the Lord for rain, in the time of the latter rain, the Lord will make flashing clouds, He will give them showers of rain… I also remembered James 1:5 which says, "If any of you lacks wisdom, let him ask of God, who gives to all liberally and without reproach, and it will be given to him."

The next occurrences of the vision we'll focus on are all of the globes of light carried by the army of God's people changing to resemble the heavenly bodies observed earlier, above the atmosphere in the heavenlies. And within the globes, the mesmerizingly power-charged brilliant colors appearing as uncut gems. Then miraculously, the followers of Jesus literally merged and morphed, becoming those very heavenly bodied, living, uncut, gemstones. They next, simultaneously, were set into the growing mountain alongside the earlier observed heavenly bodies above the atmosphere. Here, I was reminded of Philippians 2:12-15 NIV – …continue to work out your salvation with fear and trembling, for it is God who works in you to will and to act in order to fulfill His good purpose. Do everything without grumbling or arguing, so that you may become blameless and pure, "Children of God without fault in a crooked generation." Then you will shine among them like stars in the sky as you hold firmly to the word of life… (Emphasis mine).

I also was reminded of Ephesians 2:19-22 – "Now, therefore, you are no longer strangers and foreigners, but fellow citizens with the saints and members of the household of God, having been built on the foundation of the apostles and prophets, Jesus Christ Himself being the chief cornerstone, in whom the whole building being fitted together, grows into a holy temple in the Lord, in whom you also are being built a dwelling place for God." So much revelation was revealed to me in these two Scriptures. I now suddenly knew those heavenly bodies, twinkling as if gemstones above the atmosphere were saints also, representing the great cloud of witnesses cheering us on in our faith walk that the apostle Paul speaks of in Hebrews chapters 10-11, as well as, we, the light bearing people of God, disciples of Christ, being fitted together in the mountain. Also, 1 Peter 2:4-5 emphasizes Jesus being depicted as a living stone rejected by men, but chosen by God, and that believers are like living stones being built into a spiritual house. It reads – Coming to Him as to a living stone, rejected indeed by men, but chosen by God and precious, you also, as living stones, are being built up a spiritual house, a holy priesthood, to offer up spiritual sacrifices acceptable to God through Jesus Christ. And, Isaiah 28:16 declares that God lays a tested stone, a precious cornerstone in Zion.

And speaking of the mountain, recall how The Ancient of Days led me to read Daniel 2:34-35 where it speaks of a small stone not cut with human hands striking the image and becoming a great mountain which filled the whole earth. Remember how I asked if

God was saying His Holy Mountain was the whole earth, however, I received no answer and just kept mulling it over? Here is my answer. In this vision, all of the smaller mountains merged into the largest one and it kept growing in height and width until it covered the whole earth, actually engulfing it. So yes, God's holy mountain, Mount Zion, IS the whole earth, however, WE, the saints of God, are His Holy Temple, His mountain comprised of all of His holy saints with Jesus being not only the precious chief cornerstone of it, but the builder of it, His church! In Matthew 16:13-18 Jesus says to Peter, as he identifies Jesus as the Christ, the Son of the living God, you are Peter, and on this rock, I will build my church, and the gates of Hell will not prevail against it. The gates of Hell release the beast who entrances people with the wisdom of men, the wisdom of the world, however, the wisdom of God that the saints carry, is more powerful and will defeat the dark wisdom of the world! Praise His holy name!

I hear the Ancient of Days speaking and saying, "Don't be like the religious leaders of Jesus' day along with those that followed them and not understand and therefore miss your day of visitation." This can be found in Luke 19:41-44 – Now as He drew near, He saw the city and wept over it, saying, "If you had known, even you, especially in this your day, the things that make for your peace! But now they are hidden from your eyes. For days will come upon you when your enemies will build an embankment around you, surround you and close you in on every side, and level you, and your children within you to the ground; and they will not leave in you one stone upon another, because you did not know the time of your visitation."

Micah 4:1-2 – Now it shall come to pass in the latter days That the mountain of the Lord's house Shall be established on the top of the mountains, And shall be exalted above the hills; And people shall flow to it. Many nations shall come and say, "Come, and let us go up to the mountain of the Lord, To the house of the God of Jacob; He will teach us His ways, And we shall walk in His paths..."

Hebrews 12:22-24 – But you have come to Mount Zion and to the city of the living God, the heavenly Jerusalem, and to myriads of angels, to the general assembly and church of the firstborn who are enrolled in heaven, and to God, the Judge of all, and to the spirits of the righteous made perfect, to Jesus, the Mediator of the new covenant, and to the blood of sprinkling that speaks better things than that of Abel.

Once I understood all of the above, and recalled the above Scriptures, I remembered that God never showed me if the people who were lulled to sleep and slumber by the wisdom of the world were cleansed by the latter rain and joined the army of His light bearers. So, I asked Him why He didn't reveal that to me. He answered me saying, "Because that is not up to Me, it is their choice to make!" Whoa! The powerful message His answer sent, hit me hard! I know I will continue to pray over it. Ephesians 5:14 – "…Awake, you who sleep, Arise from the dead, And Christ will give you light." Ezekiel 33:11 – "…As I live, says the Lord God, I have no pleasure in the death of the wicked, but that the wicked turn from his way and live. Turn, turn from your evil ways! For why should you die…"

After that, I recalled Joel 3:14-17 – Multitudes, multitudes in the valley of decision! For the day of the LORD is near in the valley of decision. The sun and moon will grow dark, And the stars will diminish their brightness. The LORD also will roar from Zion, And utter His voice from Jerusalem; The heavens and earth will shake; But the LORD will be a shelter for His people, And the strength of the children of Israel. "So you shall know that I am the LORD your God, Dwelling in Zion My holy mountain…"

Now that you know what on earth is happening, you get to choose the role you'll have in it all. I hear the Ancient of Days reminding me to tell you all again…

THE TIME IS NOW!

LETTER FROM THE AUTHOR

Dear reader,

First and foremost, I want to thank you for taking the time to read my book. I cannot thank you enough for your support. The reason I wrote it is because long ago when the Spirit of the Lord asked me if He could use my life as an open book for Him, I answered with a heartfelt and resounding yes. I couldn't say no after all He's done for me, how He transformed my life and made me new. Since then, He has led me by His Spirit to write what was on His heart in correlation to what He has done in my life, and for that, I give Him all the glory. I wish to assure you that as a woman of God, I have yielded myself to the leading of the Holy Spirit and have faithfully written down those things He has shown and spoken to me.

If you don't know the Lord as your personal Savior, I commend you for reading this far and encourage you to seek Him out. I believe you are still reading because the Holy Spirit of God is gently and lovingly calling your name. I know that it's hard to put down our pride, to let go of trying to be the master of our own life, and to go against the grain of those around us. One thing I know most assuredly though, is that He loves you deeply, with a love that no love on earth can even compare to. Therefore, it is my wholehearted prayer for you, that you recognize He has a plan for your life so much better than you could even think or imagine, and that you accept His invitation. As you ponder over the things you've just read, may God be with you and bless you, and lead you by His Spirit. It would be an honor to call you my brother or my sister in Christ.

If you are a believer and already know what I spoke of above, I thank you for reading this far as well. My heartfelt prayer for you is that as you ponder over what the Lord showed me and led me to write, you would find peace in the midst of this darkness and chaos as He expands your understanding, just as He did mine, as He oversees you as you go through the oil press process as He brings forth the oil of anointing from within you, as He did me. If this book resonates with you and you think of others who do not yet share our faith and believe what is written within would help, then I would be honored if you would gift them a copy. As always, I pray over every book God has led me to write, asking the Holy Spirit to lead whoever is reading it to understand what God is speaking to them individually at that moment and time.

May God bless you abundantly,

Terra Kern

Other titles from Terra Kern:

Forgiven and Not Forgotten by Terra Kern

Oasis or Mirage by Terra Kern

The Deception of 666 by Terra Kern

Journey to the Mountaintop by Terra Kern

The Children's Bread by Terra Kern

Little Jenna Jafferty series by Terra Kern

Other titles from Higher Ground Books & Media

Single, Sober & Serious by Rebecca Benston

Raven Transcending Fear by Terri Kozlowski

Our Journey of Faith by Miranda Thornsberry

It's Only a Game by Darrel Johnson

One Step(pe) at a Time by Lori (Martin) Potts Zimmerman

Revealing His Might and Power by Deanna Rodriguez

Full Gospel by Jerry C. Crossley

Music and the Holy Spirit by Stephen Shepherd

The Real Prison Diaries by Judy Frisby

One Day in May by Joanne Piccari Coleman

Shameless Persistence by Sandra Bretting

God's Whispers by Christine Nekas-Thoma

Add these titles to your collection today!

http://www.highergroundbooksandmedia.com

HIGHER GROUND BOOKS & MEDIA IS

AN INDEPENDENT PUBLISHER

Do you have a story to tell?

Higher Ground Books & Media is an independent Christian-based publisher specializing in stories of triumph! Our purpose is to empower, inspire, and educate through the sharing of personal experiences. We are always looking for great, new stories to add to our collection. If you're looking for a publisher, get in touch with us today!

Please be sure to visit our website for our submission guidelines.

http://www.highergroundbooksandmedia.com/submission-guidelines

HGBM SERVICES IS OUR CONSULTING FIRM

AUTHOR SERVICES

HGBM Services offers a variety of writing and coaching services for aspiring authors! We can help with editing, manuscript critiques, self-publishing, and much more! Get in touch today to see how we can help you make your dream of becoming an author a reality!

*****

We also offer social media marketing services for authors, small businesses, and non-profit organizations. Let us help you get the word out about your book, your projects, and your mission. We offer great rates, quality promos, consistent communication, and a personal touch!

http://www.highergroundbooksandmedia.com/editing-writing-services

Need Bulk Copies?

If you would like to order bulk copies of this book or any other title at Higher Ground Books & Media, please contact us at highergroundbooksandmedia@gmail.com.

We offer discounts for purchases of 20 or more copies. Excellent for small groups, book clubs, classrooms, etc.

Get in touch today and get a set of great stories for your students or group members.